Kahuna Magic

Other Brad Steiger books
published by Para Research

True Ghost Stories

Astral Projection

Brad Steiger Predicts the Future

Indian Medicine Power

KAHUNA MAGIC

Para Research
Distributed by Schiffer Publishing, Ltd.
West Chester, Pennsylvania 19380

International Standard Book Number: 0-914918-34-6

Previous edition published by Award Books, 1971

Typeset in 10 pt. Paladium on a Compugraphic Editwriter 7500
Typesetting by Betty Bauman

Printed by R. R. Donnelley & Sons Company
on 55-pound SRT II Paper

Published by Para Research, Inc.
A division of Schiffer Publishing, Ltd.

This book may be purchased from the publisher.
Please include $2.00 postage.
Try your bookstore first.
Please send for free catalog to:
Para Books
Schiffer Publishing, Ltd.
1469 Morstein Road
West Chester, Pennsylvania 19380

Manufactured in the United States of America.
Fifth printing, May 1987, 5,000 copies
Total copies in print, 17,500

Contents

Foreword

I had no way of knowing that I was working on such a tight deadline when I set about compiling *Kahuna Magic* under the guidance of Max Freedom Long.

Max had contacted me in 1968 and asked me if I would be interested in presenting certain of the concepts of his life-long study of the mysteries of the Kahuna, the magician-priests of Hawaii, into a single popular volume to be aimed at the mass audience. To assist me in making up my mind, he sent me package after package of books, tapes, notes and clippings. Our correspondence through letters, and especially telephone calls, became extensive.

Max was persuasive. I found that things were as he had promised: The Huna philosophy was beautiful, and it truly did seem to be a system of magic which might be practiced by any sincere seeker. I agreed to do the book.

But then I had to fit the project into my schedule of previously committed publishing deadlines and lecture appearances. Max was patient, for he knew that I would keep my promise to present an overview of his work to a much larger reading public than, at that time, had been exposed to the Huna teachings. But the grand old scholar was eighty, and the gentle proddings he sent my way indicated he knew that Time was no longer his friend.

At last I set to the task of digesting the several pounds of materials he had sent to me. When that was accomplished, I next worked at interweaving Huna research with my own thoughts, observations and research references.

In the "fullness of time," as the scriptures say, the book was delivered into Max's waiting hands. As soon as he finished reading *Secrets of Kahuna Magic,* he picked up the telephone to tell me how delighted he was with the presentation of his work, how pleased he was with the resultant product.

Within a very short time thereafter, Max Freedom Long made the final projection from his physical shell into the Greater Reality. I was grateful that his guiding beings had permitted him the opportunity of seeing the book before taking him higher on the path of spiritual evolution.

In February of 1972, the First Annual Aquarian Age Conference was held in Honolulu at the Hilton Hawaiian Village on Waikiki Beach. There were good reasons for selecting Hawaii as the site of the meeting. In metaphysical lore, Hawaii is the remaining bit of geography of a great culture (the Theosophists say Lemuria) that sank beneath the ocean; legends of several peoples state that a new and glorious age will be ushered in when East meets West in Hawaii; the state itself, with its amalgamation of several skin colors and religious creeds, serves as a physical symbol of brotherhood.

I was privileged to be a speaker at the Conference banquet. My topic, fittingly, was Kahuna Magic, the ancient psycho-religious system of the Islands. My talk was based on the monumental work of Max Freedom Long, who devoted his life to breaking the secret Huna code.

While I was in Hawaii, Rev. Eddie Kung told me that he was the son of a Kahuna who had had great healing powers. He showed me a picture of Max Freedom Long standing beside a tall rock, just a bit shorter than his own six-foot-three. The next pictures he shared with me were as old as the first, and they had captured a remarkable sequence of events. Most of the photos had been published in one of the Hawaiian newspapers.

The story, as Eddie told it, was that a god (male aspect of the *Aumakua,* the High Self) had appeared to his father and proclaimed that the rock might be used as a healing stone. Hundreds came and rubbed their sores and their ailments against the rock. Many experienced miraculous healings.

To prove that he would remain as long as the people had faith, the god appeared one night to a throng of awestruck Hawaiians and left his image on the tall rock (a photograph clearly showed a male image impressed on the surface of the stone). Later, a goddess (female aspect of the *Aumakua*) appeared for the benefit of the newspaper reporters. Although the photographers were too stunned to capture her image apart from the rock, a series of newsphotos revealed the distinct features of the goddess that had replaced her male counterpart.

After a time, as one might be assured, the Board of Health became concerned about all those people rubbing their sicknesses against the stone, possibly passing contagious diseases on to others, so they decided to take action. Bulldozers were brought in to push the rock over a nearby cliff.

But Kahuna Magic proved to be too strong for spark plugs and internal combustion engines, and mysterious things kept interfering with the work of the bulldozers. Finally, though, the High Selves grew impatient with the nonsense of the state officials, and they withdrew their powers from the stone. Eddie then pointed out a photograph that showed the rock completely free of any images, just another tall, jutting stone, once again.

Of course, as Max Freedom Long would point out, one does not need such items as a "healing stone" to bring good health. Such a device would serve only as a physical stimulus for the low self within man. A better method of insuring our good health would be our carefully sending the "proper pictures" to the High Self.

As Max would tell us, we must picture ourselves in perfect health and impress that image on the low self as a thing to send as a desire to our High Self. In this manner, the low self will create a picture of us in perfect health and project the image upward. The way the High Self answers this prayer is to materialize the picture into reality for us. Max often referred to this process as the "secret of secrets in Huna."

Understand, though, that the picture of yourself in perfect health must *not* include your illness. Too many people pray thusly: "Oh, please, heal my sickness!" With such a prayer goes a picture from the low self of you in a sick and miserable condition. At the same time, the low self might also squeeze in a fuzzy picture of you as well and healthy. But the result will be confusion, and nothing will cause the High Self to change your condition. You must believe that you are receiving perfect health. You must hold the thought of yourself as well and happy.

Max always instructed his students to make the picture of themselves in perfect health with the *mana*, the vital force. This will permit a lasting thought-form picture to be sent to the High Self. As is explained in this book, proper breathing techniques are very important in order to create powerful *mana.*

"Make and memorize the picture of you in good health with breathing in order to collect the *mana* and to give the picture enough strength to hold together while the High Self materializes it into actuality for you," Max said.

After that, you should instruct the low self to send the picture and a large amount of *mana* to the High Self, like a telepathic message. Repeat the prayer action at least once a day and continue until the answer is given.

"Have faith," Max tells us. "Tell yourself that perfect health is already given on the level of the High Self and is already real. LIVE in the picture. FEEL it. Keep your mind off your ills. This is the key to real magic. It is yours to use if you will."

The work of Max Freedom Long as expressed in his sharing of the Huna philosophy contains true secrets of real magic. These secrets are workable, practical and extremely usable. And they really are yours to use if you will. I sincerely hope that you make that decision.

Brad Steiger
Scottsdale, Arizona
May 11, 1981

Introduction

"I have been able to prove that none of the popular explanations of kahuna magic will hold water," said the large bald-headed man behind the desk cluttered with botanical specimens.

"It is not suggestion, nor anything yet known in psychology. They use something that we have still to discover, and this is something inestimably important. We simply must find it. It will revolutionize the world if we can find it. It will change the entire concept of science. It would bring order into conflicting religious beliefs.

"Always keep watch for three things in the study of this magic. There must be some form of consciousness back of, and directing, the processes of magic—controlling the heat in fire-walking for example. There must also be some form of force used in exerting this control, if we can but recognize it. And last, there must be some form of substance, visible or invisible, through which the force can act. Watch always for these, and if you can find any one, it may lead to the others."

Dr. William Tufts Brigham's long white beard, bushy white eyebrows, and plump pink cheeks made him appear to be a kind of scientific Santa Claus as he sat talking to the inquisitive young schoolteacher who had come to question him about the magic of the native Hawaiian magician-priests. Max Freedom Long, newly arrived from the Mainland, had been suspicious of anything that savored of superstition, but his curiosity had become aroused by guarded references to the kahunas, the "Keepers of the Secret," which he had overheard in his classrooms.

Long had been baptized a Baptist, had attended Catholic church services with a boyhood friend, later had studied Christian Science,

Theosophy, and all religions whose literatures were available to him. He majored in psychology in college and he obtained a teaching job in Hawaii in 1917. Although he found the Hawaiians open and friendly, he was quick to discover a realm of secret and private activities which lay behind native life and resisted the curiosity of an outsider. The kahunas had been outlawed since the early days of the Christian missionaries and all activities of the native "Keepers of the Secret" were forced to be strictly *sub rosa* so far as a white man was concerned.

But the tales of healing through the use of magic, slaying through sorcery, and the charting, changing and manipulating of the future through mysterious rituals had fiercely whetted the intellectual appetite of the young academician. Rebuffs only recharged his interest to explore whatever avenues existed to lead him to a greater understanding of the kahunas.

Max Long talked to a young Hawaiian who had been educated and who had thought to show his superior knowledge by defying a local native taboo against entering a certain ancient temple. His demonstration of applied knowledge versus taboo had cost him the use of his legs. He had been forced to crawl from the temple to a plantation to seek medical help, but only a kahuna had been able to remove the potent curse.

Max read the diary of a Christian minister who had challenged a local kahuna only to have the native priest promise to pray the congregation to death one by one. The minister's diary reported how the members of his flock had begun, one by one, to perish and how the surviving members had deserted the Christian magic. Then, according to the minister's daughter, the clergyman had gone into the forests and learned how to use the magic employed in the death prayer. The kahuna had not expected such an attack and had taken no precaution against a reversal of his magic. The native priest died in three days.

The survivors of the clergyman's flock rushed back to his church, but the minister was never again the same. He knew that he had employed the tools of the kahuna, not the Church's Christ, to defeat a native magician. He attended a mission conference and scandalized his orthodox colleagues. The minister was removed from his position, but a local princess gave him land on which to live and the understanding Hawaiians built him a new church of coral stone.

Max Freedom Long's quest for more information about the secrets of the kahuna came close to bordering on the obsessional, but he found it nearly impossible to find anyone who would speak to him about the native magicians in any depth.

"I asked some of the older white men of the neighborhood what they thought of kahunas, and they invariably advised me to keep my nose out of their affairs," Long remembers. "I asked well-educated Hawaiians and got no advice at all. They simply were not talking. They either laughed off my questions or ignored them."

Then Max Long heard about the curator of the Bishop Museum, Dr. William Tufts Brigham, a man who was said to have devoted most of his years on the Islands to delving into things Hawaiian. Long went to the museum fully expecting the curator to confirm his suspicions that the rumors about kahunas were simply superstitiously exaggerated accounts of clever native witchdoctors who employed power of suggestion and skillful use of herbal poisons. Instead, Dr. Brigham fixed Long with a stern glance, mumbled something about his scientific standing, then asked Long if he could respect a confidence.

Long assured the curator that whatever he might say would go no further, then he waited for the man's pronouncement.

"For forty years I have been studying the kahunas to find the answer to the questions you have raised," Dr. Brigham said. "The kahunas do use what you have called magic. They do heal. They do kill. They do look into the future and change it for their clients. Many were impostors, but some were genuine."

Long half rose from his chair, then sank back into it. Dr. Brigham had knocked the underpinning from the world he had braced almost to solidity over a period of three years. He had confidently expected an official negation of the kahunas, and he had told himself that he would be able to wash his hands completely of them and their superstitions. Now he was back in the trackless swamp and up to his nose in a mire of mystery.

"I did not realize it until weeks afterward," Long recalls, "but in that hour Dr. Brigham placed his finger on me, claiming me as his own, and like Elijah of old, preparing to cast his mantle across my shoulders before he took his departure. He told me later that he had long watched for a young man to train in the scientific approach and to whom he could entrust the knowledge he had gained in the field—the new and unexplored field of magic."

Dr. Brigham once told Max Long that he should not feel discouragement over the seeming impossibility of learning the secret of magic.

"Just because I'll never know the answer is no reason why you will not," the eighty-year-old scientist told his student. "Just think what has happened in my time. The science of psychology has been born! We know the subconscious! Look at the new phenomena being observed and reported by the societies for physical research. Keep at it everlastingly. There's no telling when you may find a clue or when some new discovery in psychology will help you to understand why the kahunas fashioned their various rites, and what went on in their minds while they observed them."

Max realized that time was against their quest, and he feared that the sand was almost certain to run out before a breakthrough in research might occur. The kahunas had failed to interest their sons and daughters in taking the training and learning the ancient lore that had been handed down under vows of inviolable secrecy only from parent to child. Those who could heal instantly or who could fire-walk had been gone since the year 1900.

As Max took over the materials collected by Dr. Brigham during a period of forty years' research, he began the slow work of trying to find remaining kahunas and do what he could to learn the secret from them. He found it quite easy to amass a number of anecdotes detailing the wonders of the kahunas, but his greatest difficulty lay in attempting to gain an introduction to the kahunas who had performed the magic. The few remaining kahunas had learned by past unfortunate experiences to shun the whites, and no Hawaiian dared to bring a white friend to a kahuna without express permission, and that was almost never granted.

Four years after Max had met Dr. Brigham, the scholarly curator died, leaving the earnest young schoolteacher with a weight on his heart and with the frightened realization that he was perhaps the only white man in the world who knew enough to continue the investigation of the native Hawaiian magic that was vanishing so rapidly. Max Long knew that if he failed, the world might lose for all time a workable system of magic that could be eternally valuable to humanity.

Max Long ceased to make any kind of progress, and in 1931, he admitted defeat and left the Islands.

Then, in 1935, while living in California, he awakened in the middle of the night with an idea that led directly to the clue which was eventually to give the answer to kahuna magic. Both he and Dr. Brigham had overlooked a clue so simple and so obvious that it had continually passed unnoticed.

The kahunas must have had names for the elements in their magic. Without such names they could not have handed down their lore from one generation to the next. As the language they used was Hawaiian, the words must have appeared in that language. The missionaries had begun formulating a dictionary of Hawaiian-English words as early as 1820—the dictionary that was still in use. Since the Hawaiian language is made up of words built from short root words, a translation of the roots will usually give the original meaning of a word; therefore, if he could find the words used by the kahunas in their recorded chants and prayers, he would be able to make a fresh translation which would disclose secrets overlooked by disinterested missionaries.

The next morning, Long recalled that the kahunas had taught that man had two souls. Such a belief had been regarded as an absurdity and a dark superstition, but he hunted up the two words (*uhane* and *unihipili*) naming the two souls in his copy of the old dictionary that had been published in 1865. Here he discovered that the outstanding feature of the *unihipili* was that it seemed to be connected with the arms and legs of the physical body, and yet was a spirit. The *uhane* was a spirit, but it was a spirit that could talk even if it were little more than a shadow associated with the "person of the deceased." (Soon Long would add yet another spirit, the *Aumakua*, "the older, parental, utterly trustworthy spirit," the High Self.)

Here, in Max Freedom Long's own words, is how he deciphered the meaning of the root words in these designations of man's two souls:

> Both are spirits (root u), and this root means to grieve, so both spirits were able to grieve.
>
> But the root *hane* in *uhane* means to talk, so the spirit named in this word could talk. As only human beings talk, this spirit must be a human one. That raises the question as to the nature of the other spirit. It can grieve, and so can animals. It may not be a man who can talk, but at least it is an animal-like spirit that can grieve. The *uhane* cried and talked weakly. In the dictionary note it was said to be considered nothing more than a shadow connected with the deceased person. Evidently it was a weak and not very substantial *talking* spirit.

Unihipili, with an alternate spelling of *"uhinipili,"* gives more roots to translate. Combined we get: A spirit which can grieve but may not be able to talk (u); it is something that covers up something else and hides it, or is itself hidden as by a cover or veil (uhi); it is a spirit which accompanies another, is joined to it, is sticky, and sticks or adheres to it. It attaches itself to another and acts as its servant (pili); it is a spirit which does things secretly, silently and very carefully, but does not do certain things because it is afraid of offending the gods (nihi); it is a spirit that can protrude from something, can rise up from that something, and which can also draw something out of something, as a coin from a pocket. It desires certain things most earnestly. It is stubborn and unwilling, disposed to refuse to do as told. It tinctures or impregnates or mixes completely with something else. It is connected with the slow dripping of water or with the manufacture and exudation of nourishing water, as the "breast water" or milk of the mother (u in its several meanings).

To summarize, the kahuna idea of the conscious and subconscious seems to be, judging from the root meanings of the names given them, a pair of spirits closely joined in a body which is controlled by the subconscious and used to cover and hide them both. The conscious spirit is more human and possesses the ability to talk. The grieving subconscious weeps tears, dribbles water and otherwise handles the vital force of the body. It does its work with secrecy and silent care, but it is stubborn and disposed to refuse to obey. It refuses to do things when it fears the gods (holds a complex or fixation of ideas), and it intermingles or tinctures the conscious spirit to give the impression of being one with it.

Given this certainty that the kahunas had known for thousands of years all the psychology we had come to know in the last five years, I became quite sure that their ability to perform feats of magic stemmed from their knowledge of important psychological factors not yet discovered by us.

Max Freedom Long had resumed his search for the "Huna," the secret so long guarded by generations of devoted "Keepers." He proceeded with the monumental task of presenting the Huna system of magic in all its details and in amassing all available proofs of its correctness as a workable set of scientific facts. This volume will serve as an introduction to Long's work and his contention that Huna might be a system of magic which might be utilized by everyone.

In a series of paperback presentations, I have sought to introduce to the mass audience the research and lives of unique men and women who have developed philosophies or conducted investigations which I feel are deserving of wider dissemination than within their personal clientele or their individual study circles. In this present volume, the research and applied metaphysics are those of Max Freedom Long, who devoted most of a lifetime to a study of the mysteries of the kahuna, the magician-priests of Hawaii.

As in previous volumes, my approach is that of unbiased reporter. I am not attempting to champion or to sell any of these metaphysical systems of dealing with the cosmos. I am only interested in providing the syntheses which may afford a wide readership the opportunity to familiarize themselves with ideas which might otherwise have remained forever unknown to them. It is up to each individual to accept or to reject the essentials of the philosophies which these paperbacks present.

At this point, I feel it pertinent to repeat a brief statement of intent which has come to serve as a kind of creed for me and my work:

> I do accept the reality of nonphysical man, and I do hold that man is more than chemical reactions, glandular responses, and conditioned reflexes; but you will have set yourself a difficult task if you should attempt to pin me down to any one approach, any single school of thought, or any specific dogma.
>
> I feel that I must remain eclectic in my approach to the world of the paranormal if I am to be of any real service to my readers. The moment I believe too strongly in any one theory, then I shall attempt to force every encountered scrap of psychic experience into that pet hypothesis. If this should occur, my objectivity would be destroyed and I should become worthless as an investigator. I should become the "true believer" and not the searcher, the explorer of the strange, the unusual, and the unknown, who sets forth on his voyage into the paranormal with an open and inquiring mind.
>
> Surely, the psychic field—perhaps more than any other—requires objective reporters. Books on subjective philosophies and metaphysical journeys abound. Should there not be room in the investigation of the paranormal for the open-minded searcher, the writer who allows his readers to make up their own minds concerning the merits of psychic experience?

The open-minded reader should find a good many stimulating concepts for perusal in this book. Some may find certain of the theories a bit controversial, even heretical, while others may discover that they have the ability to make practical applications of some of the psychic "secrets" revealed by the kahunas.

Brad Steiger
September, 1970

1

Hawaiian Words Used in Huna Magic

aha, or *aho*, a spiritual thread or cord.

aka, shadowy outline or form.

aka-lua, shadowy body.

akua, a god.

anana, the "death prayer."

ano, seed.

atua, a god.

Aumakua, the High Self.

hane, to cry or wail as a spirit, from roots *ha* and *ne*, to talk in low voices.

haoles, white people.

hini, small, weak, to speak.

ho-ano, to reverence.

hoo-la, or *hoo-ola*, to heal.

hoo-mana, to worship.

huna, secret.

ka, a spiritual cord.

ka-ka, a cluster.

kala, to cleanse.

kaula, a prophet.

kino, body.

kino-aka-lau, having many shadowy bodies.

kino-wailua, a ghost.

la, light.

la-ko, a supply.

lau, spread out, many.

lele, to take flight.

lomilomi, manipulation.

luau, a native feast.

maikai, good.

makaula, a prophet, mystic.

mana, vital force.

mana-loa, strongest vital force.

mana-mana, to branch out or divide.

mana-o, to think.

Nahini, Woman of the Skies.

nihi, to abstain from acts because of fear of gods.

papa, forbidden.

pau-lele, to trust in.

pili, to adhere or cleave to.

poi, a native food.

taro, food root.

ti or *ki,* plant used by kahunas.

uhane, middle self.

uhi, cover or veil.

unihipili, low self or subconscious.

wahini, woman, female.

wai, water.

wai-lua, ghost.

wale, to be, to exist.

wawae, the leg and foot.

In the pronunciation of Hawaiian words, the sound of the vowels is that used in Latin. *A* as in father; *E* as long *a* in ale; *I* as long *i* in isle; *U* as *oo* in moon; *O* as long *o* in over; *W* almost like *v*. *Uhane* is pronounced oo-hah-nay. *Unihipili* is pronounced oo-nee-hee-pee-lee. *Aumakua* is pronounced Ah-oo-mah-koo-ah.

2

How Huna May Be a Workable System of Magic for Everyone

For centuries the kahunas have practiced a system of magic so powerful as to enable them to control winds and weather, to foresee the future and to change it to pray their enemies to death, to heal the sick instantly, to walk unshod over hot lava, to read minds, to raise the dead, to send and receive telepathic thoughts...the list is almost endless.

With the advent of the white man and his religion, however, the kahunas began their decline. Western culture could not compete with the kahuna on his own terms, so it successfully limited his practice, legally, through the power structure. In scarcely a generation the natives had overwhelmingly embraced Western culture, along with its style of dress and its religion.

If there are any practicing kahunas on the Islands today, they are most likely very old and living in isolated corners. The missionaries arrived in Hawaii in 1820. From a living, practicing cult, Huna has now been reduced to an esoteric study.

But Huna has not changed. The laws that made Huna operable two hundred years ago are still in existence, and, according to Max Freedom Long, the knowledge of how to work those laws can still be learned. For although the kahunas took their secrets with them when they died, they could not take their language. The Hawaiian tongue, through the painstaking work of Max Freedom Long, has been forced to yield its secrets. Linguistic analysis of the words used by the kahunas to describe their rites has enabled Long to discover the psychic principles employed by the Hawaiian priests.

Max Long claims that these psychic principles can be employed by anyone today who takes time to learn them and who has the patience to develop them. Huna offers the reasons behind the phenomenon so that the student, when told to concentrate, knows what is taking place in his head, both physically and psychically.

Dr. William Tufts Brigham postulated three things to look for in the study of magic: first, there must be some sort of consciousness manipulating the magical operation; second, there must be some kind of force used to sustain this manipulation; third, there must be some medium through which the force can act.

In Huna, it is said, one can know and name each of these three vital elements and effectively utilize them. If one understands the *why* of something, it is much easier for him to see the *how* of it. Since a large part of magic consists of convincing oneself that he is actually doing something out of the ordinary, the more details he can understand about the process, the better.

The Hawaiians did not need to be persuaded to believe in the reality of what we would call paranormal occurences. A man of the 1970's, however, trained by a scientifically oriented society to think in tangibles, needs physical proof that he can offer to his powers of reason and rationalization. He cannot be told an object is blue; he must have pigments explained to him. He cannot be told telepathic communication is possible; he must first understand the physical laws that make it possible.

When the kahunas instantly healed the sick, they knew what was happening to the diseased area. Excellent psychologists as well, they also knew, in many cases, how their clients' minds were affecting both the illness itself and the cure. Without these psychological insights into their patients, the kahunas would have been considerably crippled in their healing efforts.

Students of the occult scene today find themselves crippled by some of the nebulous teachings afoot in the field. One is told to send out a thought telepathically "until contact is made." When the bewildered student wonders how he will know when contact is made, he is blandly assured that he will "just know." Granted there are many excellent teachers of psychic development, but oftentimes the most psychically endowed are virtually inarticulate on the ways and means they use to achieve their admirable results.

In Huna the student is told to instruct his low self to travel along the *aka* cord connecting himself and the target for the mental communication until the target has been reached. Since he understands the mechanics of telepathic linkage, the result is that he has more psychic ammunition with which to convince himself that what he is doing is not only possible, but that he himself is doing it.

The necessity for sustaining self-belief in order to achieve any kind of success has caused many a Doubting Thomas to declare that psychism or magic is all in one's head. When a particular act involves more than one person, "suggestion" is the usual explanation. While it cannot be denied that belief and suggestion play extremely large roles in the successful working of magic, Huna shows how these two factors are not the total substance of magic, but are merely used to trigger the actual processes of such things as healing, telepathy, and precognition.

Before going any further, I think a clarification of terms is in order. A standard dictionary defines magic as "the pretended art of producing effects beyond the natural human power by means of supernatural agencies or through command of occult forces in nature." Ignoring for the moment the blatant bias of "pretended," we have a definition for acts committed beyond the scope of the human mind *as we know it.* The dictionary bases its "pretended" on the scientific dogma that declares that *we cannot prove the mind capable of such feats, therefore such feats do not exist.*

Necromantic aspects aside, I believe most "magic" will be proven within the range of human power once science understands the mechanism of these "magical" processes. To do so, however, the scientist would have to remove the limitations he has placed on the human mind. He would first have to concede that such things as telepathy, psychokinesis, and instant healing are possible, then learn the laws that govern them.

The Huna system of magic would seem to provide an excellent springboard into the mechanics of psychism, for what the kahunas did worked, and they had reasons why it worked. Perhaps the light of modern psychology would find certain errors in the priests' logic, but the results of their magic indicate that the kahunas knew enough of the human mind to make it perform acts we cannot consciously duplicate. If psychism occurs in members of our society, it is through the accident of birth or it is acquired through years of training and development.

In Hawaii, Huna was not accessible to everyone. The priests jealously guarded their secrets, passing them on only to blood children. Nevertheless, had they so decided, they could have taught it easily to the natives. Max Long believes that one need not have any natural psychic abilities in order to successfully practice Huna, nor does one need to painstakingly develop these abilities before being able to practice Huna. Huna is simply a system that allows for psychic development in the natural course of its practice.

The bulk of Huna material deals directly with the laws that make psychic feats possible, or the why of them. The kahunas believed that one first had to be acquainted with the tools with which he was working. One should be thoroughly based in the philosophy behind the system before attempting to apply it. It is in the successful application of Huna principles that, in a natural way, psychic abilities are triggered.

Huna works because of the priests' understanding of man and his component parts. In accordance with Dr. Brighams's criterion for magic, the system contains a form of consciousness, directing the magical processes; a force utilized by the consciousness, providing the necessary power; and some substance, visible or invisible, through which the force can act. These elements the kahunas believed to be inherent in man.

The kahunas did perform some of their magic with the aid of spirits of the dead, most notably the death prayer. Such practices would fall accurately under a definition of magic as Mr. Webster sees it, for they make use of "supernatural agencies." In this chapter, however, let us confine our discussion to magic within the scope of human mind power. The death prayer, spirit intervention, and other acts involving deceased spirits will be covered in successive chapters.

Huna magic could perhaps more accurately be called a system of psychology. To be able to successfully "work" Huna magic, one simply needs to know the component parts of man, as conceived by the kahunas, and understand how they relate to each other. As in a chess game, only specific moves are allotted each piece.

The kahunas saw man composed of ten elements. The most startling additions to most readers will be the inclusion of two souls, for the kahunas believed each man to have three souls, or spirits, residing in him. These three souls he called *unihipili, uhane,* and *Aumakua.* It was the roots contained in these words that gave researcher Long his first clues to their functions in Huna.

When root words and overlapping syllables were put together, Long came up with a spirit that grieves, but cannot talk; attaches itself to another and is subservient to it; acts secretly, silently, carefully; and is hidden. *Unihipili* was thus described.

An astute psychologist should recognize from the clues given in the root words that the *unihipili* referred to the subconscious. This knowledge gave the kahunas a couple centuries' jump on modern psychology, which did not discover the subconscious until the close of the last century.

One should not, however, assume that the kahunas were merely personifying the subconscious by calling it a spirit. Kahuna beliefs clearly state that the *uhane* and *unihipili* are two separate spirits inhabiting one body. The two spirits, or selves, work as a team, for each has functions that rely on the abilities of the other; and each needs the physical medium of the body.

The *Aumakua* translates as "older, parental, utterly trustworthy pair," implying that it is composed of a male and a female essence. This dual spirit has both the low self (*unihipili*) and the middle self (*uhane*) under its guidance and protection. It occupies the level of consciousness immediately above our own conscious level, and it corresponds to the superconscious in psychology. The *Aumakua*, called the High Self, does not require sacrifices or bribes, yet it was the highest "god" with whom the kahunas ever dealt. They believed in a supreme creative force, but they did not believe that they could pray to it. The only level of consciousness they felt they could humanly comprehend was the one in which they were dwelling. Their only contact with the level directly above their own was due to their connection with the High Self.

Surrounding these three spirits, or selves, according to Huna belief, were three invisible or shadowy bodies. These shadowy selves correspond to the etheric and the astral doubles of occult literature. These amorphous bodies, made up of what the kahunas called *aka* substance, form a sheath, or cloak, in which the three souls of man reside. There is one sheath for each respective soul, with varying degrees of density. *Aka* has been likened to ectoplasm, and it will be discussed in greater detail in the chapter on telepathy, in which *aka* plays an essential role.

Thus far the kahunas have presented us with three souls and three invisible bodies for these souls. To perform feats of magic, however, some form of operable force would also have to be present. The kahunas were not only aware of this force, but they effectively controlled it in all their rituals.

Huna argues that each body of man has its own supply of *mana*, or what we would call vital force. In Hawaiian terminology, the low self operates with simple *mana*, the middle self uses *mana-mana*, or a higher voltage, and the High Self uses *mana-loa*. The voltage used by the High Self is so supercharged that it has atom-smashing properties.

Long presumes these three voltages to be electrical, although proving it in a laboratory may be as difficult as securing the biblical manna that fell from the skies to feed the Israelites in the wilderness. Low *mana*, however, can be likened to body waves, which can and have been recorded scientifically. Likewise, *mana-mana* may correspond to brain waves. Science has not as yet provided us a counterpart for *mana-loa*.

The kahunas taught that *mana* was created by the low self from the body's daily intake of food. Within the low self's domain *mana* can flow from person to person, or from animate object to inanimate object. Low *mana* is controlled by will. *Mana* manifests as will on the middle-self level giving us a repetition of the roles played by these two spirits in relation to themselves. The conscious mind uses *mana-mana* to form all its thoughts. The middle self can thus instruct the use of *mana* in the low self and direct the low self's contact with the High Self.

The High Self has an incredible amount of power. The power to control temperature was demonstrated by the kahunas in their fire-walking activities, and their manipulation of physical laws was evidenced in their capacity for instant healing. The resources of the superconscious lie largely untapped in modern man, but there is no reason why he cannot learn to utilize them. All he must do is clear the path to the High Self and unleash its beneficial powers.

These ten elements, then—the three souls, the three shadowy bodies, the three voltages of vital force, and the physical body—comprise man as the kahunas knew him. By a further understanding of the functions and interrelationships of all component parts, the kahunas were able to develop a "psycho-psychic" system that had them practicing a very workable form of magic. To them the tools of psychology became the keys to their psychic abilities. And, though they carefully guarded their secrets, passing them on only to their children, anyone who understood the basic psychology and psychic discipline behind the secret could achieve the same results as the kahunas.

The most essential element necessary for success was, and still is, contact with the High Self. It is on this level, above our own conscious level, that the power is sufficient to perform miracles. In Huna thought, contact with the superconscious can only be made by the low self, acting under orders from the middle self. The low self is connected to the High Self by a shadowy cord, *aka*, made of the same substance as the shadowy bodies. When contact is desired, it is achieved by the flow of *mana* up the aka cord until the High Self is reached.

Unfortunately, it is not unusual for blockage of some sort to appear, making contact impossible. This blockage, unless it is caused by spirit intervention, occurs on the subconscious level.

The kahunas believed the low self to be the seat of memory in which is stored all the thought forms created by the middle self. According to the Hawaiian system, thoughts really are things. Each thought becomes a tiny bead of *aka* substance which clusters around other thoughts of a similar nature. When a specific piece of information is required by the middle self, it simply instructs the low self to produce the necessary information. The whole cluster is reviewed, explaining why memory is associational.

The low self is also the creator of emotions. Within it are formed such emotional responses as fear, guilt, and pride. It is guilt, however, and all the attendant emotions associated with it that concern us here, for they are the emotions that inhibit contact with the High Self. If the low self does something of which it is ashamed, it will try to avoid the High Self, much as the naughty child, either stricken with remorse or fearful of punishment, will seek to avoid its parents.

Guilt and fear become such fixed thought forms in the low self that every time the middle self instructs the low self to contact the High Self, it will collide with these emotions and stubbornly refuse to make contact. In this way the individual often finds himself at the mercy of his unreasonable subconscious self. Today an individual faced with this problem would go to a psychoanalyst. In Hawaii, years ago, he would have gone to a kahuna. The kahunas were well aware of this recalcitrant aspect of the subconscious.

Often, treating an illness meant the removal of this complex, as we would call it, held by the low self. Once more they were ahead of modern psychology in their understanding of psychosomatic illnesses and maladies related to hysteria.

This matter of complexes was considered so widespread that if one were to visit a kahuna today, a complex would be the first thing the kahuna would try to unearth. No matter what the individual's problem might be, the kahuna would wonder why the person had been incapable of solving it himself. The kahuna knows the High Self to be capable of anything. Therefore, if the client's High Self has not solved the problem, the kahuna immediately suspects some kind of blockage. And if something is interfering with the normal intercourse between High Self and lower selves, the kahuna knows the culprit to be a complex.

Just what significance does this talk of High Selves, low selves, complexes, contact, and *mana* have for modern man? Translate the Hawaiian terms into psychological jargon, become cognizant of the fact that fifty percent of all hospitalized patients in the United States are mental patients, and the answer should begin to focus.

Once again the "magic" used by the kahunas—to heal in this case—shows itself to be a coupling of the laws of psychism and psychology.

When the kahunas were at their best in Polynesia, they taught the people to live without hurting others. Those who willfully hurt others were considered worthy of death, and were frequently punished with the death prayer. The kahunas had no need for lengthy dogmas, or commandments. Their one simple rule was to live without hurting another. If such were to occur, one immediately sought forgiveness. If one neglected such an act, one was in danger of eventually slamming shut the door between low self and High Self.

With the advent of Christianity, the kahunas found themselves treating a host of complexes resulting from the supposed "sins" set down by the church. The doors in these people were closed, the paths blocked, through no responsibility of their own. There had been no injury to another person.

It is to these church-created supposed sins that many who suffer from a lack of confidence, depression, negativism, and a host of other contemporary maladies can trace their difficulties. These people need to realize that their spiritual worth lies beyond the restricting confines of institutionalized science and religion. Huna is one way to effect this realization. In Hawaii, the successful person was one who was on intimate terms with himself. He was one who understood the relationships between his three composite souls and who was in good rapport with his High Self. The three elements functioned as a highly efficient unit and the person was careful to do nothing that could upset this delicate balance.

The kahunas taught these truths to their people long before they reached Polynesia. According to their perfectly preserved oral tradition, the Polynesians came from a homeland blessed with "heavenly dew," which had been overlooked by mountains. Nothing in the legend yields the specific geographical location of the homeland, however, nor is any reason given for migration of the several Polynesian tribes.

Efforts to trace the path of migration through the language used by the Polynesians have been made by a number of able scholars, but nothing definite has been learned, according to Max Freedom Long, other than that there are many words to be found in Africa that are duplicated in the tongue of the New Zealand branch of the migrants, the Maoris. Research has also discovered that an excellent dialect of the Polynesian general language is spoken on about half of the large island of Madagascar, off the coast of Africa. Finally, Judge Fornander, long a resident of Hawaii and student of the native culture, decided that the Coptic language of ancient Egypt more closely resembled the Hawaiian than any other.

The final, official decree from the anthropologists declares that the eleven Polynesian tribes originated as a small coastal tribe of fishing peoples in South China, were driven out by stronger tribes and forced to find new homes in the Pacific. They were supposed to have reached the far islands by being blown away from land while fishing in their dugout canoes. None of this explains how, when the missionaries landed on Hawaii's shores, her people already knew the story of the Christian Creation, the Fall, the Flood, even the story of Jonah and the whale.

This last bit of information led the early missionaries to conclude that either the Devil or some renegade Christian monk or priest had given the Hawaiians the stories. The theory, however, did not explain why the Polynesians were completely ignorant of the story of Jesus. Researcher Long could only conclude that somewhere along the line the Polynesian tribes had been in contact with people who knew the Old Testament. Their migration, then, must have commenced before Jesus was born.

Long received what he considers to be the most intriguing clue to the Polynesians' origin from an Englishman, Reginald Stewart. In about the year 1900, Stewart discovered a small Berber tribe living in the Atlas Mountains of North Africa that possessed the secrets of the Hawaiian kahunas. Their queen was the last of a long line of kahunas, and she told him of the legend preserved in the tribe which stated that their people had lived long before in Egypt and had helped build the pyramids with their skill in the use of magic. Eventually the tribe had moved west to find a new home. At the same time that this Berber tribe moved west, the legend states, eleven other tribes of the same people had left by way of the Red Sea to find new homes in the Pacific, which had been seen in visions.

Before this woman's accidental death, Stewart had been placed under her tutelage to learn the ancient magic. He kept his notes, and a later analysis of the words in the "special language" she had used to teach him were recognized as a dialect similar to modern Tahitian.

The question of the origin of the Hawaiian people remains a matter of speculation. And, to some, the question of the effectiveness of the kahunas will always be a matter of speculation as well. Others will dismiss all magic as hocus-pocus sleight-of-hand used to manipulate the superstitions of the primitive mind.

When the missionaries arrived in 1820, the high priest was a man named Hewahewa. Had it not been for his tragic error in judgment, the kahunas might still be healing the sick, changing the future, and rendering other impossible services to mankind.

Hewahewa served in the time of Kamehameha I, and the high priest helped the great king to unite the islands under one rule. When the conservative old king died, Hewahewa began to look into the future. What he saw intrigued him greatly. He saw white men and their wives arriving in Hawaii to tell the Hawaiians of the white man's God. He saw the exact spot on a certain beach on one of the eight islands where the white man would land to meet the native royalty.

To a high priest this was most important. Evidently Hewahewa had made inquiries of the white seamen then in the Islands and had been told that the white priests served Jesus, who had taught them to perform miracles, even to raising the dead, and that Jesus himself had risen from the dead three days. One can imagine the tale being properly embroidered for the benefit of the Hawaiian priest.

Convinced that the white men had superior ways, guns, ships, and machines, Hewahewa took it for granted that they had a superior form of magic. Realizing that concentration had overtaken temple Kahunaism at the time, Hewahewa promptly decided to clear the stage for the arrival of the white kahunas. He acted at once, and the temples were all in ruins when, on an October day in 1820, at the very spot on the beach that Hewahewa had pointed out to his friends and the royal family, the missionaries from New England came ashore.

Hewahewa met them on the beach and recited to them a fine rhyming prayer of welcome he had composed in their honor. In the prayer he mentioned enough of the native magic—in veiled terms—to show that he was a magician of no mean powers, then went on to welcome the new priests and their "gods from far high places."

Official visits with royalty completed, the missionaries were assigned to various islands with permission to begin their work. Hewahewa elected to go with the group assigned to Honolulu. He found himself in a tight corner, however, for it soon developed that the white kahunas possessed no magic at all. They were as helpless as the wooden gods that had been burned. The blind and sick and halt had been brought before them and had been taken away, still blind, still sick, and still halt. Something was amiss. The kahunas had been able to do much better than that.

It developed that the white kahunas needed temples. Hopefully, Hewahewa and his men set to work to help build a temple. It was a fine one made of cut stone, and it took a long time to complete. But when it was at last done and dedicated, the missionaries still could not heal, to say nothing of raising the dead, as they were supposed to do.

Hewahewa had fed the missionaries and had befriended them. His name had appeared frequently in their letters and journals. But, soon after the church at Waioginu was finished, his name was erased from the pages of the missionary reports. He had been urged to join the church and become a convert. He had refused and, we can only suppose, went back to the use of such magic as he knew, and ordered his fellow kahunas back to their healing practices.

The Christians could not compete with the kahunas on the Hawaiians' own terms, so they took a short cut through the power structure and had the kahunas legally outlawed. The law reads:

Section 1034. Sorcery—Penalty. Any person who shall attempt the cure of another by practice of sorcery, witchcraft, *ananna, hoopiopio, hoounauna,* or *hoomanamana* (terms describing the practice of Hawaiian kahunas), or other superstitious or deceitful methods, shall, upon conviction thereof, be fined in a sum not less than one hundred dollars or be imprisoned not to exceed six months at hard labor.

There is also another section of the law which defines the kahuna as one who takes money under the pretense of magical power. For this offense the fine goes up to a thousand dollars and a year in prison.

Kahuna lore, however, could only be passed on from parent to blood child, and with the onward rush of the twentieth century, the old kahunas could not get their children to take the arduous training. Kahuna practice is for all practical purposes dead in Hawaii, which is why men like Max Freedom Long are so concerned about spreading the word of Huna to the people.

3

How the Kahunas used the Great Ha Prayer Rite

The correct use of the *Ha* prayer rite enabled the ancient kahunas to contact the intangible something that answers prayers and, literally, from our perspective, performs miracles. The secret of their success lay in the kahunas' ability to reach and to enlist the aid of their High Selves. Max Freedom Long says that this rite can be used by anyone who earnestly desires to learn how it is done, and who correctly follows the format prescribed by the kahunas.

According to Huna psychology, the conscious or middle self cannot of itself approach the High Self. This is something only the subconscious can do, provided there is no blockage. The role of the conscious self is to instruct the low self to accumulate an extra supply of *mana*, which is to be held in readiness until the next steps have been taken. Then the subconscious, again acting under the orders of the middle self, reaches up the connecting *aka* cord and makes contact with the High Self. It is this High Self that brings about the desired conditions expressed in the prayer, although the prayer itself is brought about only by the integrated efforts of the three composite selves.

Before presenting the four basic steps in the *Ha* prayer rite, two additional elements must be stressed. These are consistency and repetition. It is important for the High Self to receive a clear and unwavering picture of the situation or object desired through the prayer. If it picks up the contradictions and fragments of a constantly changing image, it will become confused and its efficiency will be greatly decreased. Morever, the constant image should be continually fed to the High Self. The rite should be used daily until the individual is satisfied with the results.

In order to keep the image as clear as possible, the individual must carefully choose the prayer he wishes to make. He should know in advance what image he intends to send to his High Self. If he has done the work of deciding these things before the actual work of the prayer is undertaken, he should not have to worry about sending a confused request.

Once the prayer has been formulated, the practitioner is ready to begin. There are four basic steps:

First, the middle self instructs the low self to create an extra amount of *mana*. This is done by taking four deep breaths. These breaths should be taken in very slowly; they are much like the deep-breathing exercises of the yogis. Once this *mana*, or vital force, has been aroused, it is held in readiness.

In *The Huna Code in Religions*, Max Freedom Long explains the code meaning of the command to take four deep breaths before practicing the *Ha* prayer. The secret, he says, is to be found in the several code meanings of the names for the numbers 1, 2, 3, 4; or *kahi, elua, kolu*, and *kauna* or *ha*. According to Long:

Ka-hi is "one." This word, as the maker of the dictionary explains, was often used in place of one pronounced at times in almost the same way, *ka-he*; both have the meaning of "to cut longitudinally" (split open), which was, with the Huna people, "to circumcise." Behind this strange custom of circumcision, which has spread around half the world and which even the Australian Arunta people practiced, lies the secret meaning of sacrifice—the sacrifice of a part of the creative or life force. The male sex organ was symbolic of this creative force, and with many ancient peoples the circumcision rite was one of great importance. It was accompanied by special acts and, with some tribes, was part of the initiation of a boy into the estate of manhood.

It is most interesting to find that there was no definite reason given in the Bible where, in Genesis 17:10-27, God was said to have spoken to Abram, ordering him to establish a new covenant between his people and their God. In this covenant all males were to be circumcised, but no reason was given for the command. One suspects the reestablishment of an older custom, or the borrowing of one from some other religion. The Huna system would seem to be the most likely source as it was evidently older, and as it gave in its secret word code a reason for the practice.

This reason is to be seen in the code words and their roots. *Oki* is "to cut," and *omaka* is the "foreskin." That gives the outer meaning. The code meaning comes from the secondary meanings of the words or roots. To cut is also *kahi*, meaning (1) the Number One; (2) a place; and (3) the pronoun, one. As "cut" it has the meaning of "opening," and in the alternate word, *kahe*, the secondary meaning is "a flow of blood." The thing to be opened by cutting, and with the accompanying flow of blood, is the *omaka* or foreskin, but this word also means "the fountainhead of a stream of water" (water symbolized mana), and in this we have the secret. The covenant was one established in Huna with the godlike High Self, and the creative force or mana was to be sent as a gift or sacrifice. The cutting, foreskin and blood flow stand as outer symbols for a pact or pledge to supply the High Self with the mana it needs to perform its part of the work of living—living as part of the three-self man. Perhaps no better example can be found of the misunderstanding of a Huna code teaching, and its blind use in outer form, than that of circumcision. We see clearly that the Ha Rite of prayer, starting with the count of "one," calls for the accumulation and sending of mana to the High Self, certainly not for the actual cutting of the foreskin. (The women kahunas were on a par with the men, and sent mana to the High Selves in the usual way, and they, naturally, were not circumcised.)

That the rite was very ancient is shown by the traditional use of a flint knife for circumcision. In Egypt the religious aspect of the rite was very clearly outlined in the fact that Horus, son of Osiris and Isis, died and was resurrected as a part of the Mystery of Amenta, and was shown then in his statues and paintings as circumcised. The Mohammedans borrowed the rite from the Israelites and used it, but in India and China, if practiced, circumcision had no religious significance. Only in Yoga is there a trace of the belief that the life force is connected in some way with the male sex organs, for "serpent force," or *prana*, was supposed to originate in the genitals, rise along the spine and pass out through the top of the head during the performance of elaborate breathing exercises (*pranayama*) which were accomplished by mental visualizations. The Yoga practitioners believed that the *prana* (mana) they accumulated was drawn from the air. The kahunas seem only to have known that the heavier breathing made the accumulation of extra mana possible. In modern times we would say that the extra oxygen taken in was used to burn blood sugar already circulating in the blood stream, and thus make of it the vital force. It is evident that in Yoga there was once a knowledge of the Ha Rite, but that as time passed, the reason for accumulating mana was lost. In "arousing the serpent force" it came to be sent from the body through the "Door of Brahman" or top of the head, but after leaving the body its destination became Supreme God, not the "Father" or High Self.

Getting back to the code word, *ka-hi* once more, we find in the root, *hi*, the secondary meaning of (1) "to flow away," and (2) "to be weak." This would tell us little if we did not already know that it was the mana which flowed like its symbol, water, and that the flow was directed at the time of making the Ha Rite prayer to the High Self, which is "weak" if not supplied with the mana. Those initiated into Huna learn that this mana-sending "covenant" between the lower pair of selves and the High Self is to be observed daily, without fail, and its observation marks the initiate as one above the lower ranks.

The code also places in *kahi*, for "one," two other significances for the initiate. The three-self man becomes "one" when the contact with the High Self is made in performing the Ha Rite. The meaning of "a place" is better understood if we look for the "place" to which the flow of mana is directed—the place of the High Self.

E-lua or *A-lua* is "two." The root *alu* also means "weak," and so we have a repetition of one code meaning in the number "one" (it was a common practice in presenting the code to use more than one word to repeat the inner meaning lest it be overlooked). The same root, *alu*, means "to combine"; "to aid or give assistance"; and "to adhere." These meanings point to the combining of the three selves in the prayer work and the "adhere" idea symbolizes the low self, which is described in its name, *unihipili*, as something that adheres to something else, or, in its case, to the middle self. By calling attention to the low self in this way the reminder is given that the low self is the one which, on command, accumulates the extra mana, reaches out along the *aka* cord to contact the High Self, and sends the flow of mana.

The root, *e* in *elua*, the alternate word for "two," has the meaning of (1) "to call or invite attention," which codes the low self making contact with the High Self; (2) "something strange or new," and this description fits the High Self, especially when the root, *e*, is doubled to make *ee*, which means "something out of sight."

An odd but important signficance is to be found in the meaning of *alu*, "to break or crumble to pieces." This codes the Huna belief that the future is automatically made for us by the High Self out of the shadowy substance, in a "pattern world" on its level. It is made to match our plans and hopes and even fears. When we decide to ask in prayer for quite a different future, the High Self must break up the patterns already formed and begin to build them again to fit the prayer.

The roots *lua* and *lu* give us "seeds" and "to scatter seeds" as in sowing them. The belief here is that when we pray for something, we must make a mental picture of the desired thing or condition, and that this picture is composed of tiny thought-forms or ideas impressed on microscopic bits of the *aka* substance by the low self. These clusters of thought-forms are the "seeds" which must be sent floating with a flow of mana to the High Self, and if accepted, are then symbolically watered with mana and made to begin to grow into the thing which will be the "answer" to the prayer.

Ko-lu is "three." Again we have a repeated root carried from the preceding number, *lu*, for "scattering seeds." But in the root *ko* we have the sign of the possessive case which tells us in code that in making the prayer we must exert faith and believe that what we have asked has been built already in the pattern world by the High Self. We are reminded of the words of Jesus, ". . . believe that ye receive them, and ye shall receive them."

The root *ko* also means "to accomplish; to fulfill; to bring to pass," and this tells us the part played by the High Self in the answering of prayer. There is also the meaning of "to create; to beget; to obtain what one has sought after." The High Self creates the patterns of the changed future for the man, and gradually brings about the new conditions.

Ha, for "four" means "to breathe strongly," and this gives us the method of accumulating extra mana. It also means "a trough" for running water, symbolizing the sending of the flow of mana to the High Self.

Kau-no, the alternate word for "four," gives us the root, *kau*, and this has great value in the code because of its many meanings, one of which is, "to place something in a designated place," and in which we see the idea of placing the mana and thought-form "seeds" of the prayer in the keeping of, or place of, the High Self. The meaning of "to set before one, as food" points to the offering of mana to the High Self. Another meaning is "to fall upon; to embrace affectionately," in which we have the code for the love shown the lesser man by the High Self. The 17th meaning listed in the dictionary is "to rehearse in the hearing of another that he may learn," this giving us the idea of repeating the prayer often and without changing it. The 22nd meaning is "to place and then to rest," which describes the action taken in making the prayer, the mana and thought-form picture being "placed" with the High Self, and the completed action then stopped or rested.

It is of interest to note that after the elaborate pains taken by the kahunas in placing the special code meanings in the names for the first four numbers used for counting, the following numbers drop the code completely. If we count on to "five" we find in *elima* only the secondary meaning of "a hand" indicating the use of five fingers and the hand in primitive counting. In "six" we have *e ono*, with only the secondary meaning of "something pleasant to eat." Going on to "ten" to conclude the ten-finger count, *umi*, the secondary meaning, certainly does not apply to the Ha Rite of prayer. It is "to choke" as in using both hands to choke an enemy.

The second step in this Hawaiian rite is also executed by the low self, under orders from the middle self. With the accumulated *mana* still residing in the lower self, the subconscious reaches up along the shadowy *aka* cord until the High Self has been successfully contacted.

When this contact is assured, the low self releases its store of *mana* as a kind of sacrificial gift to the High Self. The High Self will use this vital force to formulate the answer to the prayer.

Finally, rising up the *aka* cord with the mana is the mental image of the thing desired by the individual.

Repetition of this rite is so necessary that it should be considered a fifth step. And not only should the clear picture be continually projected, but so should the daily supply of *mana. Mana* strengthens the High Self. Without *mana* the High Self would be too weak to accomplish anything in this conscious plane in which we live.

Another way to accumulate an excess amount of *mana* in the lower self was taught by Baron Eugene Ferson, now deceased, who lectured widely on magnetism and its effects. The "mana" of the kahunas and the "magnetism" of Ferson seem to have achieved the same sort of results.

Ferson taught his many pupils to stand in the "star position," feet wide apart, arms extended at the sides, level with the shoulders. Next, the students were to repeat the affirmation: "The universal life force is flowing through me now...I feel it!"

Max Freedom Long believes that if one were to add the four deep breaths of Huna to this exercise, a considerable supply of *mana* could be realized for use by the High Self.

As already indicated, the initial formulation of the prayer is essential to the success of the *Ha* prayer rite. The attitude one develops pertaining to the prayer is also of vital importance. Man has been told in innumerable sources that "whatsoever things ye desire, believe that ye have them and ye shall have them." This element of belief is also of great importance in successful application of the *Ha* prayer.

Throughout the actual rite the individual must rest in the quiet faith that the High Self is already taking care of the request.

The Hawaiians frequently illustrated this faith with the metaphor of the seed. Just as one could plant a seed, see it grow into a plant, then pick the fruit, so should one envision the path taken by one's specific prayer. The seed must be trusted to eventually bear fruit. The length of time involved would simply depend upon the nature of the request, some changes requiring considerably more time than others.

Two other factors, in addition to lack of belief, may interfere with the success of this prayer rite, namely guilt and spirit intervention. A sense of guilt imbedded in the subconscious inhibits its contact with the High Self. The High Self is always willing to give aid to the two lower selves, but if the subconscious does not feel worthy of any assistance, it will be afraid to approach its mentor. Sometimes this situation results from an actual sense of wrongdoing, while more often it is like the child who desires punishment—expiation—for his "sins."

Spirit intervention is a difficult subject to explain to Western readers, but the kahunas firmly believed the low self could actually be prevented from making contact with its High Self if either had been strongly influenced or possessed by evil spirits. The Hawaiian concept of spirits will be dealt with more fully in succeeding chapters.

In order for a prayer to be successful, one must look to the request and to the motivation. The Hawaiians were emphatic in their belief that the High Self—the "utterly trustworthy parental pair"—could perform no ill to anyone. The two lower selves, regrettably, have this failing, but if they choose to harm someone, it is an action divorced from the High Self. The *Ha* prayer rite cannot be successfully employed if the supplicant desires harm—physical or emotional—to another. The seed will atrophy.

The *Ha* prayer rite works because the High Self has the ability to change the future. This is what prayer is all about, for if one wishes to change a certain condition, it is because he is convinced that that unappreciated condition shows no sign of changing itself, but will continue its undesirable course into the future. The High Self daily builds the future of the individual, using his mental images as tools. This is why the formulation of goals is so important, for, obviously, if a consistent image is projected, a consistent future will be constructed. But if the only tools the High Self has to work with are a jumble of impressions, the pattern it creates will show a corresponding confusion.

One employs this knowledge of the future-changing ability of the High Self when one carefully chooses the prayer, then faithfully repeats it every day. The kahunas believed that thoughts were things, in that they were composed of the same *aka* substance as the three shadowy bodies. Thus, each time the prayer is formulated, it becomes a microscopic "bead" on an *aka* thread. For each repetition a duplicate bead is made, and the stronger becomes the strand.

The Huna system may possibly explain the mechanics of the "positive thinking" approach, which teaches one to constantly project a positive mental attitude. Huna may also cover a myriad of other psycho-psychic approaches to creative problem-solving. Max Freedom Long believes that Huna has the advantage over all other systems, however, for in Huna, one knows *why* he is doing something and *how* it works.

4

How the Three Souls of Man Direct the Force of Huna

"If the kahunas were right in their idea that human consciousness is composed of two separate spirits on this level, with a third or superconscious spirit acting as a guardian angel, so to speak, we have in that concept an addition to psychological knowledge which is of such importance as to be hard to estimate," Max Freedom Long has observed.

It is Long's contention that such a concept should cause man to reexamine the more orthodox religious theories of the human soul. If the kahunas were correct in assuming that we have within our spiritual makeup a less-evolved lower spirit newly risen from the animal kingdom, as well as a more evolved spirit that has long been removed from the animal kingdom, our orthodox ideas of salvation will also have to be restructured. Two salvations will be necessary rather than one, for if we accept the knowledge of Huna, we accept the spiritual inclusion of two souls, each at a different level of development. The metaphysical concepts of karma and reincarnation will also have to be revised in the same way and for the same reason. Two unequally developed souls will require two separate reincarnations and two separate applications of the divine law of karmic responsibility and spiritual evolution.

Max Freedom Long argues that under the older and more workable system of Huna, man may come to see himself in a clearer light. "We may trade simplicity for the triplicity of being," he admits, "but orthodox Christianity has accustomed us to consider God a triplicity. Apparently, we have lost sight of man as a similar triplicity."

In Huna doctrine this complication becomes easier to grasp if one always keeps in mind the fact that the low, animal spirit within us, the *unihipili*, does all the remembering for us, but has inferior powers of reasoning. Our conscious-mind spirit, the *uhane*, is unable to remember for itself, but it can use the full power of inductive reason.

Psychical research has recognized four main classes of ghosts and apparitions:

1. Experimental cases in which an agent has deliberately attempted to make his apparition appear to a particular percipient.

2. "Crisis-apparitions" in which a recognized apparition is seen, heard, or felt when the individual represented by the image is undergoing a crisis, especially death.

3. "Postmortem apparitions" in which a recognized apparition is seen or heard long after the person represented by the phantom has died.

4. Ghosts or apparitions that habitually appear in a room, house, or locale.

On the other hand, the kahunas have classified several kinds of spirits and arranged them in categories quite new to us of the West:

Kinds of Ghosts or Spirits Listed According to the Kahuna Lore

1. The ordinary normal spirit of one deceased. This spirit is made up of a subconscious and a conscious spirit, as in life. It thinks and remembers like any ordinary normal living man. It uses the same forces.

2. The subconscious spirit of a man, cut off from its conscious companion by some accident or illness before or after death. This spirit remembers very well indeed but is illogical, having only animal-like deductive reason. It responds to hypnotic suggestion. It is like a child and is often a playful "poltergeist" or noisy ghost. It loves to attend seances and make tables tip. It tries to answer questions, and usually gives such answers as make it appear to be a liar or worse. It loves to imitate one's deceased relatives.

3. The conscious mind spirit of man, cut off from its companion subconscious spirit before or after physical death. This spirit cannot remember, therefore it is a nearly helpless wraith, wandering about aimlessly, sometimes making its presence known, sometimes seen psychically, but acting the part of the true "lost soul" until rescued

eventually and paired off again with a subconscious spirit who can furnish it with remembering powers—often with a set of memories of a former life in which the rescued conscious spirit or *uhane* had no part.

4. Spirits of the superconscious order, including what may be called "nature spirits or group souls," after the Theosophical terminology. Only vague information is given as to this class of spirits, although it is concluded that they frequently take a hand in the activities of the two lower spirits, the *unihipili* and *uhane*, helping them to do things of a spectacular nature at times.

Max Freedom Long maintains that the best proof of the kahuna theory of the three selves and of their different forms of mentation is to be found in checking multiple-personality cases with cases of obsessional insanity or schizophrenia.

In the first-mentioned form of mental phenomenon, Long theorizes, the patient remains sane while obsessed or controlled by a normal ghostly intruder with distinct subconscious and conscious selves, and able, therefore, both to remember and use reason. "Only personality (conscious self) may change, or only memories may change (subconscious self), or both may change—but still there is sanity because a reasoning conscious self is always in control of the body regardless of mental changes," Long says.

In cases of obsessional insanity, mental aberration results from the changes because the conscious self is displaced and a new one does not take over the body. This leaves the resident subconscious in charge, and lacking reason, it keeps the body alive but in a condition of lack-of-reason, or insanity. Or an invading subconscious self may obsess or take over the body after the resident two selves have been driven out.

Cases of insanity are common in which a foreign subconscious self obsesses a body. We know that it is foreign because it brings with it a foreign set of memories and convictions, even when illogical. The insane who believe themselves to be Napoleons are of this type, often not dangerous, often being able to remember from day to day, but never able to use the type of reason characteristic of the conscious self.

The important thing to understand is that the kahunas believed that there were three separate and independent spirits, and that these were known to be separate and independent because they could be separated by accident or intention.

Of only slightly less importance is the knowledge that the subconscious alone can remember, and that only the conscious can reason, while the superconscious has a still higher form of mentation which gives it exact knowledge of the past, the present, and the part of the future that has been determined in advance.

5

How the Kahunas Practiced Telepathy and Mind Reading

As has already been explained, the kahuna system gives one three units or measures of magic: first, the consciousness at work in any given operation; second, the force used; and third, the invisible substance through which the force operates, through which this electrical type of energy is conducted and brought into play. Furthermore, there are three spirits or selves in the composition of man, each self having its own peculiar mental powers, and each using its own particular voltage or vital force.

It is the three additional elements of man—the three shadowy or etheric bodies of man—that complete the picture and play such an essential role in the subject to be discussed in this chapter, telepathy.

The priests of Hawaii believed that man has three bodies made up of an invisible substance that serves each of man's three spirits as a ghostly body. These vehicles presumably exist before the birth of the physical body and after its death. The Hawaiian term for these bodies is *kino* (body) and *aka* (shadowy). The *aka* body of the low self is densest in quality and the superconscious is finest.

Aka has the additional meanings of being a luminous extension away from the body, or a circle of light around the moon or sun before it rises above the horizon. This image can be applied to man's etheric bodies, for the kahunas taught that the bodies of the conscious and subconscious spirits blend with the living physical body, interpenetrating it. They have the power to come and go. The shadowy body of the superconscious spirit also interpenetrates the entire body, but it has the added quality of being a mold of every cell, bone, and tissue of the physical body.

The two lower selves reside with the physical body. The High Self, or *Aumakua*, does not. It is connected to the two lower selves by a cord made of the same substance of which the etheric bodies are made, *aka*. This *aka* cord corresponds to the "silver cord" known to astral travelers and mediums. Contact is maintained by the flow of *mana*, or vital force, between the two points.

The kahunas found other uses for the low self's ability to construct connecting threads of *aka* substance. They believed that all things, be they humans, animals, flowers, chairs, or thoughts, have shadowy bodies. Moreover, these bodies remain after the objects in their gross physical form have been destroyed. What is of importance here is the priests' belief that thoughts have shadowy bodies, that they are substantial and enduring things.

The process of thinking, the kahunas believed, creates thought forms. And, as most thoughts come in a train and in relation to other thoughts, the shadowy bodies of thoughts (thought forms) group in clusters. These clusters were symbolized in the Huna system by bunches of grapes.

The phenomenon of mental telepathy has been fairly well established in most people's minds. There are still those who insist that mind-to-mind contact without the benefit of sensory interaction is impossible, but the majority of people realize that it is even more impossible to place such restrictions upon human mind power. They are justified, however, in wanting to know why telepathy works, and how it works.

A number of theories have been developed by capable researchers in the field of parapsychology in an attempt to formulate an explanation. Dr. Milan Ryzl, a parapsychologist of some repute, has released statements that can admirably be applied to Huna. "Initially," Ryzl has reported, "ESP proceeds in the same way in which other sensory perceptions are apprehended; information on the object to be cognized is coded into signals, which are then carried to the subject by an as yet hypothetical medium. At this point the ESP process undergoes regularities that are exclusively parapsychological.

"Granted certain favorable circumstances, created by the receptible state of the subject's mind, these signals are then able to call forth a corresponding reaction in the neuropsychical processes of the subject. They either give rise to an unconscious—physiological—reaction, or they become manifest as a conscious experience, the characteristics of which are formed by the subject's psyche."

Remarkable experiments have been conducted with primitive peoples to test the hypothesis that telepathy is an archaic means of communication, which, although remaining as a vestigial function of mind, was once the sole method for conveying ideas.

It has been observed that the primitive bushmen in Australia can accurately transmit thoughts, feelings, and ideas to friends and relatives several miles away. They also use "psi" abilities to locate missing objects, straying cattle, and thieving enemies. The bushmen live a Stone Age existence. Their normal sensory abilities have been heightened by their struggle for survival. Their eyes can identify objects at great distances without the aid of field glasses. Their powers of smell are probably on a par with those of a sensitive collie. Their ESP talents are even more remarkable.

The Australian anthropologist, Dr. A. P. Elkin, of Sydney University, was forced to rearrange some of his scientific thinking after he had conducted some studies among the bushmen. In his *Aboriginal Men of High Degree*, Dr. Elkin writes that although his arrival was never announced by messenger, drums, or smoke signals, each village was prepared for his arrival, knew where he had just come from, and was aware of the purpose of his wilderness trek.

Whenever the anthropologist heard of a case where a native claimed to have gained personal information telepathically from a faraway village, subsequent investigation proved the knowledge to be accurate. Whether the information concerned a dying parent, the birth of a nephew, or the victory of a successful hunt, the recipients' knowledge of the event was completely in accordance with the actual happening.

Dr. Elkin was told: "Thoughts, though invisible, can be sent flying through the air."

In controlled experiments, Sydney University psychologist Ronald Rose found that the Australian bushmen consistently averaged better than fifty percent correct in dice-guessing tests. In one particularly impressive test, the psychologists placed a cigarette in a tightly sealed box. Three bushmen were asked to guess what the box contained. One, slightly more sophisticated than the others, promptly told the researchers that the box contained a cigarette. The other two guessed that the box contained "tobacco and paper."

To increase the difficulty of the experiment, a cigarette holder was placed in the box and ten natives were chosen at random to guess the contents. Admitted separately to a sealed hut, the aborigines quickly responded to the challenge placed before them by the psychologists. Although none of them had ever seen a cigarette holder before, nine of them precisely described the shape, length, and color of the unknown object.

The kahunas believed that there are threads of shadowy body substance connecting friends who send telepathic messages back and forth. These *aka* threads are perfect conductors of vital electrical force. With this in mind, Dr. Ryzl's "as yet hypothetical medium" may be proven someday to be the etheric matter identified by the Hawaiians as *aka*. The "neurophysical processes" may apply to the way in which *mana*, or vital force, travels along interconnecting *aka* threads.

As a result of experiments with "body waves" and "mind waves," we have come to know that the vital force is electrical in nature and that it flows or leaps in small charges along our nerves and from cell to cell in the body. Such voltage was reported by Drs. Libet and Gerard of the University of Chicago to be a millionth of a volt less in the brain cell interchanges, but the action of the charges was that of "million-volt potentials of current."

Not only did the kahunas believe that the vital force passed unimpeded over *aka* threads, they maintained that the flow of current could transmit thought forms to make complete messages or impressions.

"As a subconscious spirit has control of all threads of shadowy body substance," Long explains, "all thought forms after they are created in the course of 'thinking,' and of all flows of the low *mana* or body electricity,' we cannot send and receive telepathic messages at will. We must give the subconscious a mental order to do the sending and receiving for us, then relax and wait for it to set to work. We can tell it what messages to send, but we can only wait for it to receive messages and push them to the center of consciousness so that we can become aware of them. This process is similar to that of recalling a memory, in so far as any sensation accompanying the receiving of a message is concerned."

According to Huna theory, in order to make contact with the person whose mind is to be read, the subconscious self must first cast out a thread of the *aka* or shadowy body stuff to connect itself with the subconscious of the person with whom communion is desired.

It is the Huna belief that the subconscious has the strange and marvelous ability to project a portion of its shadowy body in much the same manner as an amoeba projects a part of its body to make a "hand" with which to grasp a particle of food.

In telepathy or mind reading, the kahuna practitioner will first visualize, or project, a "hand" being formed and extended toward the person he wishes to contact.

Upon reaching the subject, it becomes necessary to "pierce" and to enter the shadowy body of the person, just as a spear would pierce a physical body.

The telepath must remember that, according to Huna theory, the subject, if aware of an effort to touch and to pierce through his invisible body, can usually cause his subconscious to repel such an approach. This can be accomplished by an effort of the will of the subject's middle self or conscious mind. Hypnotic suggestion may be repelled by the same action on the part of the middle self.

Once contact has been made with a subject who does not resist, a thread of shadowy stuff connects the two individuals. Along this thread travels a flow of the low *mana* of the vital force.

When the telepath has become connected in this way with his subject, he has joined them with an electrically charged invisible cord. Now the subconscious of the telepath may project a tiny part of its sensory organs to the far end of the cord and observe what thoughts are passing through the mind of the subject. The subconscious is thus able to duplicate these thoughts as thought forms in their individual shadowy bodies and send them back on the flow of vital force to the telepath's center of consciousness. Once this has been accomplished, the thoughts of the subject are presented to the focus of consciousness of the middle self (much as a memory is presented by the low self when desired) and they become known to the telepath proper, who is the middle self.

"It took me years to dig out the hidden meanings of the words used by the kahunas and to see at last just what takes place," Max Freedom Long has stated, referring to the steps in kahuna mind reading and telepathy detailed above.

"The first and most important thing to understand is that the low self has in its shadowy body duplicates of every cell and issue of the physical body, thus duplicating all sensory organs."

Laboratory tests have indicated a number of interesting facts concerning the conditions under which telepathy—and, in general, all testable "psi" phenomena—works.

Distance seems to have no effect on telepathy or clairvoyance. Equally remarkable results have been achieved when the percipient was a yard away from the agent or when the experimenters were separated by several hundred miles. Dr. S. G. Soal, the British researcher who has conducted extensive tests with "mind readers," has written:

"In telepathic communication it is personality, or the linkage of personalities, which counts, and not spatial separation of bodies. This is what we might expect on the assumption that brains have spatial location and spatial extension, but that minds are not spatial entities at all.

"If this is true, then there is no sense in talking about the distance between two minds, and we must consider brains as focal points in space at which Mind produces physical manifestations in its inter-action with matter."

"Psi" researchers have learned that the percipient's attitude is of great importance in achieving high ESP scores. Personalities do enter into "psi" testing even as they do into other aspects of human relationships. A cheerful, informal atmosphere that is as un-laboratory-like as possible encourages the successful functioning of ESP. It has also been demonstrated that those who "believe" in their "psi" powers score consistently higher than those skeptics who regard it all as a lot of nonsense.

Although the agent in the laboratory must be careful to create and foster a friendly and cheerful atmosphere, spontaneous "psi" seems to work best under conditions which Dr. Jan Ehrenwalk terms a "state of psychological inadequacy." Naming this state of "psi" readiness the "minus function," Dr. Ehrenwalk believes that "a necessary condition for telepathic functioning is a state of inadequacy or deficiency such as loss or clouding of consciousness (sleep, hypnosis, trance, fever, brain defects)."

The "psi" researcher faces another risk in the laboratory when he is engaged in the long-term testing of a percipient: the decline effects in ESP that can be brought on by sheer boredom in the method of testing. The exercise of "psi" ability does sap psychic energy and even excellent performers invariably score higher when they are fresh. Once the novelty of the test has worn off, the interests of the percipient wander elsewhere, and so, apparently, does the ESP. Once again one is reminded of the difficulty of forcing "psi" into the laboratory in strenuous attempts to satisfy orthodox science's demand for controlled and repeatable experiments.

6

Astral Projection
in the Huna System

Those remarkable journeys in which the mind travels outside the body are known as out-of-body experiences (OBE), or astral projections. Dr. J.B. Rhine, world-famous parapsychologist and head of the Foundation for Research on the Nature of Man, is said to have records of some ten thousand such cases which have been received from people all over the world. How many undeclared experiences exist may never be known, but OBE is neither as uncommon nor as far out as one might suppose.

Dr. Eugene E. Bernard, professor of psychology at North Carolina State University, has conducted research on OBE and admitted that he believes in the reality of the phenomenon. In fact, Dr. Bernard claimed that he personally experienced OBE on three different occasions.

Dr. Bernard told Thomas Leach of the *Chicago American Magazine* that, from his study to date, he would estimate that one out of every one hundred persons has experienced out-of-body projection. "It doesn't seem to be confined to any one sex, age range, or economic scale," the psychologist said.

Dr. Bernard compared the phenomenon to "...lying on a sofa, getting up, and seeing your body still lying on the couch." According to Dr. Bernard and other researchers, the mind may remain in the same room or be projected thousands of miles away. The separation of spirit and body may last from a few seconds to a few hours.

In an interview with Rob Wood of the Associated Press, Dr. Bernard said that he had uncovered one case in which an individual had an out-of-body experience while sitting at his desk. The subject's mind was projected to a city that the subject had never visited. Upon the reunion of the subject's mind and body, the astral traveler was able to describe in detail a street, an office building, and the persons whom he had seen at work within the building. Dr. Bernard said he had personally investigated and had found the street, the building, and the people.

As with nearly all other psychic phenomena, the psychologist has learned that OBE most often occurs "...during time of stress; during natural childbirth; during minor surgery, and at times of extreme fear."

Among those who have undergone OBE, Dr. Bernard found a certain number who have developed the ability to make their mind leave their body at will.

Dr. Bernard and other parapsychologists who have taken a special interest in astral projection have confirmed the hypothesis that OBE is as universal as other psychic phenomena. Completely unrelated individuals from every state, country, and cultural influence have described the same patterns in out-of-body mind travel.

"It is improbable that so many people who are apparently psychologically healthy are having hallucinations," Dr. Bernard commented to journalist Leach. "There is still much we don't know about the mind and its abilities. I don't know how long it will take, but I believe the astral projection theory can be proved and controlled."

If out-of-body experience could be established to the satisfaction of the scientific community, the textbooks of the physical sciences would have to be rewritten. The implications of such academic acceptance of OBE are staggering and would reach into every area of human endeavor. Religion, philosophy, psychology, and medicine, as well as physics, would come in for some vital revisions.

In 1952, Dr. Hornel Hart submitted a questionnnaire to 155 students at Duke University. Dr. Hart asked this question: "Have you ever actually seen your physical body from a viewpoint completely outside that body, like standing beside the bed and looking at yourself lying in bed, or floating in the air near your body?"

Thirty percent of the students answered yes to this question. After extensive studies of several other student groups, Dr. Hart concluded that at least twenty percent of college-level young people believe that they have experienced some sort of astral projection or out-of-body experience.

Dr. Hart's conclusions were enthusiastic about the staggering aspects of scientifically established OBE. "Suppose it could be proved in even one conclusive case that a full-fledged personality observed and functioned fully at long distances away from the physical brain which it normally used; or suppose that, in even one conclusive case, it could be shown that such an apparition functioned in the described way after or while the brain which it normally used was physiologically dead, then the central biological denial of survival would break down."

In the opinion of the majority of the scientific establishment, no "one conclusive case" has yet been produced by the parapsychologists. Absolute, objective proof, which will satisfy every skeptic, may never be provided in this area which deals with "whatsoever is deepest and most unitary in man's whole being."

Max Long has commented:

> The difference between mind-reading and astral travel is dependent on how much of the low shadowy body is projected. If only a small part is projected, the center of consciousness remains in the physical body, which contains the mass of the low shadowy body. But if the mass of the low shadowy body is projected, leaving only a thickish thread of shadowy substance to connect it with the physical body (astral cord), the center of consciousness necessarily moves with the greater part of the shadowy body and becomes actually present at the distant place which is visited.

> This brings up the matter of being able to remember what has been seen after returning from the astral travel journey. Huna explains how memories are made—and so far we moderns have no other explanation to consider. A memory is a thought which has been preserved by being in some way impressed on a microscopic particle of the shadowy body substance.

> Creating a thought seems to be possible to all three spirits of man, as well as to animals and even lower forms of life. All thinking is done by means of vital force of some voltage. As each thought is formed, it is given its shadowy body and is fastened by a thread of the same substance (or by direct contact, perhaps) to thoughts which came before or after it (association of ideas in terms of modern psychology is thus explained).

> When a thought has been created and impressed on its bit of shadowy body substance, it is taken by the low self and stored in that part of the low shadowy body which usually interpenetrates those sections of the brain which we know are related to the act of remembering. In our normal and waking conditions, these thought forms are actually in the tissues of the brain, and when the middle self

desires a memory, such as a friend's name, the low self finds it in the place where it is stored in the combined brain-shadowy-body brain-duplicate-origin and presents it to the middle self to be sensed. Memories are recalled in chain form, associated memories being presented as they are dragged up with the memory desired.

For instance, when we remember the name of a chance acquaintance, we also remember how he looks, how his voice sounds and where we are accustomed to seeing him. Memory can be increased by careful attention to these associated ideas or thoughtforms. The kahunas, we remember, spoke of these associated thought forms as "clusters"—clusters as of berries or grapes. A bunch of grapes seems to have illustrated the mechanism very well in that each grape is fastened to a stem, the stems to a central stem, and this to the vine and its root, and to the earth, and through it to all other things rooted in the earth.

The fact that vital force is used in the process of thinking has been well demonstrated through the experiments with the body and brain waves. These are not waves as in radio projection—a very important point to us—but are confined to the body very closely. Graphs made of the movement of waves or tiny electrical discharges through nerve and other tissues of the body show that when one is asleep there is a different graph marked on the charts. This indicates that the low self uses a different voltage of vital force in a different way in its thinking during sleep and dreams. The most marked and irregular graphs are caused by the combined thinking of both the low and middle selves during waking hours. During unconsciousness the needle of the recording machine shows almost no electrical action, allowing the graph lines to flatten out completely.

The mechanism of projection of a part or of the main mass of the shadowy body (low or combined with the middle as in conscious astral travel) is something which will bear close study. At the present stage of this investigation upon which I am reporting, it cannot be said just how one is able to project a thread of shadowy body substance across the room, or the whole shadowy body mass across half a continent. The best guess seems to be that the magnetic nature of shadowy body stuff, when charged with vital force, and acted upon by the consciousness, results in the use of attraction or repulsion as a motive force. By analogy we can consider the action of extending a "hand"—as the kahunas did. But when the mechanism is finally understood in its fullness, magnetism may play a large part, especially when it comes to explaining the almost violent attraction exerted to jerk the astral traveler back to his body when the latter is disturbed.

In mind-reading, as in telepathy, the thought forms of one person are not taken from him by another. It is evident that duplicate thought forms are created by the very act of sensing what thoughts are present in the mind of the subject or of a fellow operator in a telepathic exchange. It is also evident that, each time we recall a memory, we create a duplicate of it in the process of considering that memory. Thus a poem is learned by repeated remembering of its lines, and a repeated reduplication of the memories of the words and lines—until all associated thought-form clusters are very strong and permanent and easily found and brought to the focus of consciousness by the low self. (Remember that the middle self cannot remember. It cannot store thought forms in its shadowy body, and, if separated at death from its partner low self, is unable to remember who or what it is or has been. It is indeed a sorry ghost in the separated condition.)

The low self stores all our memories in its low shadowy body, and after death, we are able to use those memories. They do not die with the decay of the brain tissues of the dead physical body.

7

How to Deal with the Vital Force of the Kahuna Death Prayer

There were several kinds of kahunas in Hawaii before the onslaught of the white man's civilization scattered the ancient lore. Some of these kahunas were hardly more than spiritualistic mediums. Some were gifted with precognition—the ability to glimpse the future. Some kahunas labored to control wind and weather. A few were able to perform almost any part of the magic, be it healing or controlling the elements. Among the most accomplished kahunas were those who could employ several magical abilities and who could also use the *anana*, the "death prayer."

According to Max Freedom Long, "The ability to use the 'death prayer' was based on a mechanism so strange, and to us so fantastic and incredible, that it stretches the imagination to grasp it. To become able to use the 'death prayer,' a kahuna had to inherit from another kahuna one or more ghostly subconscious spirits. Or he might, if he were sufficiently psychic, locate subconscious spirits or ghosts, and use hypnotic suggestion to capture and enslave them."

Investigation has disclosed that in very early Hawaii, prisoners of war or other unfortunates were sometimes given what apparently was hypnotic suggestion in a potent form so that their subconscious spirits, after death, would separate themselves from their conscious-mind spirits and remain as ghosts to serve as guards at sacred stone enclosures or native temples built for a decadent form of Kahunaism. It is quite likely that some of these unfortunates were given orders to serve kahunas in the *anana* before they were executed.

Those kahunas who regularly practiced the ritual of the death prayer usually had about three of these enslaved ghostly subconscious spirits at their command. When a person was to be prayed to death for any one of numerous reasons, the kahuna summoned his mesmerized spirits and gave them orders to absorb *mana* from food and drink that had been placed on the ground and surrounded by such ceremonial objects as small white stones and certain pieces of wood.

The enthralled spirits were given explicit instructions as to what they were to do with the absorbed *mana*, the vital force. They were commanded to catch the scent from a bit of hair or soiled garment belonging to the intended victim and were told to follow it as a dog sniffs a track. Once they had definitely located the victim, they were to await an opportune moment to enter his body.

Over and over the kahuna chanted his deadly order:

"O Lono,

Listen to my voice.

Rush upon (name of victim) and enter;

Enter and curl up;

Curl up and straighten out."

"The command to 'curl up and straighten out' meant something different to them than it does to us," Max Long explained. "The enslaved spirits were to enter the body of the intended victim, or attach themselves to it, and proceed to absorb his vital force and to store it in their own ghostly bodies. As the vital forces of the victim were withdrawn, a numbness came to him which started at his feet and rose gradually over a period of three days to knee, hips, and finally to the heart. Once the numbness encircled the heart, the victim would soon be dead."

Upon the death of the victim, the intruding spirits left the corpse, taking with them their newly absorbed charges of vital force. If the victim had been rescued by another kahuna, the invading spirits might have been sent back to their master with fatal results. In order to avoid such a boomerang of the death prayer, the kahuna usually observed a ritual cleansing.

In some cases, the more ethical of the kahunas demanded that the person who had employed them to send out the death prayer take an oath that the intended victim was deserving of such drastic punishment and, should another kahuna accomplish a reversal of the magic, that the client alone would be held responsible by the attacking spirits. In those instances when the enslaved spirits returned to their master upon the completion of a successful mission, the kahuna would command the spirits to play until they had used up the vital force which they had stolen from the deceased victim. Such spirit recreation usually took the form of the phenomena known as poltergeist activities, in which objects would be thrown about in violent explosions of energy.

"None of the usual explanations of the death prayer, such as the use of a mysterious poison or of dying of superstitious fear, were true," Max Long declares. "Almost never did the victim know that he was about to be killed by magic."

To illustrate this point, Long relates a case which he transcribed from his notes shortly after an evening with Dr. William Tufts Brigham.

Dr. Brigham had gone to Napoopoo on the island of Hawaii soon after the museum had been built. He wanted to climb Mauna Loa to collect indigenous plants. The trip would be of three weeks' duration and he was traveling with native guides and a pack train.

Dr. Brigham had reached the barren country above the rain forests and was making for the summit crater of Mauna Loa when one of his men became ill. Dr. Brigham assumed the boy simply needed some getting used to the altitude, but when he returned to the camp that night, he found that he had real trouble on his hands. The older men had decided that the young man was being prayed to death.

Here, in Dr. Brigham's own words, as nearly as Max could transcribe them, is the scientist's account of his battle with the kahuna death prayer on the summit of Mauna Loa:

> I made another and more thorough examination, but found nothing significant except the usual symptoms of slow paralysis of the lower limbs and threatening general collapse, all of which symptoms belong to the death prayer. At last I became convinced that the old man was right and that some kahuna was at work. When I admitted this, all of the men became frightened. For all they knew the whole party might be killed.
>
> I went back to my meal and thought things over. Meantime, one of the men kept on questioning the boy. After a while he got some interesting information. The boy's home was on the windward side of Hawaii in a little out-of-the-way village in a narrow valley which ran to the sea. There was little to bring the *haoles* (whites) to the village, and

its old kahuna had endeavored to keep the people isolated and living in the old way. Among other things, he had commanded them to have no dealings with the *haoles* under penalty of being prayed to death. The boy had left home and gone to live in Kona several months back. He had all but forgotten the command.

Up to the time of my arrival at Napoopoo, the boy had lived entirely with his Hawaiian friends and had not come into contact with white men—at least not in a business way. When I was hiring men for my trip up the mountain, he had joined me without a second thought. It had not occurred to him that the command still held outside his village.

As I heard about these things I became more and more angry. My temper was no better in those days than it is now when it comes to someone injuring my friends. I sat there wishing I could lay hands on the kahuna, and also facing the fact that my work would have to stop if the boy died and I had to take him down to the coast.

While I was thinking things over, the old man came to me as spokesman for the others and made a perfectly natural suggestion. He politely called my attention to the fact that all Hawaiians knew that I was a great kahuna and even a fire-walker. To him it seemed simple enough that I should adjust matters by praying the kahuna to death and saving the boy.

The men waited expectantly, and I could see in their eyes their confidence that I would turn back the death prayer and that all would be well. On my part I was cornered. I had bluffed for years, and now my bluff had been called. I was most uncomfortable. If I refused to do the obvious thing they would be sure that I was afraid of the kahuna and not the strong fellow I pretended to be.

Now I've always had a considerable pride, and at the thought of showing what might be mistaken for the white feather before my men, I decided there and then to try my hand at sending the death prayer back to the kahuna. This is perhaps the easiest thing an amateur magician could be called upon to do. The spell had been initiated and the trained spirits sent out. All I had to do was put up the usual big arguments to talk the brainless things over to my side, and then exert all my will to send them back and make them attack the kahuna. I felt this would be fairly easy as the boy was guilty of no actual sin.

I was a long way from the *ti* leaves which are usually brushed over the victim as a part of the ceremony to help drive out the spirits, but I had never believed them very necessary. Moreover, I was angry and impatient. I got up and said to the men: "You all know that I am a very powerful kahuna?" They agreed most enthusiastically. "Then watch me," I growled. With that, I went over to the boy and set to work.

The trick of the thing is to put up an argument of such cunning that the spirits will be made to think that their master must be a devil to send them to kill one so pure and innocent. I knew that if I could win them over and get them worked up to a high emotional state and ready to revolt, I would be successful. Of course, I had to chance the kahuna having *kaola-ed* (cleaned) himself; but I thought that improbable as he would have no fear that I would send back his death prayer. I doubted if he had ever heard of me over on that side of the island.

I stood over the boy and began to advance arguments to the spirits. I was smoother than a politician. I praised them and told them what fine fellows they were, how deserving and clever. Little by little I worked around to tell them how sad it was that they had been made slaves by a kahuna instead of being allowed to go on to the beautiful heaven that awaited. I explained just how they had been captured by the kahuna and imposed upon. I told them how pure and innocent and good the boy was and how black and vile the kahuna was. I still consider that argument a masterpiece. The Hawaiians blubbered from time to time as I described the pathetic condition of the spirits.

Finally I decided that I must have the spirits ready to pull the kahuna limb from limb. I was ready to give them the command to return and visit the kahuna with ten times the punishment he had ordered for the boy. I could bull-roar in those days with the best. I can yet! (The doctor threw back his head and gave a roar that shook the house.) Well, I gave my commands in about such a tone. I yelled so loudly that I frightened the pack animals. The men drew back hurriedly and the boy whimpered like a frightened child.

It was a supreme effort, mentally, emotionally and physically with me. I put every particle of will and concentration into that command. When I had repeated it three times, I sat down by the boy, trembling and dripping.

I continued to keep my mind fastened like a vise on the project in hand, never letting it waver from my willed determination to see that the spirits obeyed my orders. The light faded and the stars came out. The boy lay silently waiting. From a safe distance the men watched me with faces now expectant and now reflecting horrible fear of the unseen. At times the air about us seemed to tremble with the fury of some unearthly conflict of forces.

The longest hour in history was about gone, when I suddenly felt an odd sensation. It was as if the tension in the air had gone in a flash. I drew a deep breath. A few minutes later there came a whisper from the boy. *"Mawae...maikai"* ("Legs...good").

I could have shouted in my triumph as I set to work to massage the twitching limbs, which seemed to react as if they had been frozen and were gradually becoming warm again. Little by little circulation was restored and the toes began to wiggle. The men crowded around me to offer timid congratulations. It was the high point in my career as a kahuna. In an hour the boy was up and eating his *poi*.

But that wasn't the end of the story. I had a pleasant conviction that I had killed something deadly. I wanted to check on my performance and see what had happened to the kahuna. I decided to cut my trip short so I could go down to the boy's village—the collecting had been less successful than I had hoped, anyway.

We covered the ground rapidly in the few days we stayed on the mountain-tops. We camped one night at the lake on Mauna Kea, and explored the crater of Mauna Loa. We roasted by day and froze by night.

In due time we pulled out for the lower country on the north side of the mountains. Water was easier to get, but the country was badly cut up and the forests heavy. At last, however, we got down to the ocean and struck a trail which took us along the bluffs and up and down through valleys and ravines. Always we followed the sea.

Late one afternoon we came straggling out of the brush into a clearing in a fair valley. An old woman and a girl were working on a *taro* patch as we came along. They took one look at me and the boy, then flew screaming before us. We followed and soon came to a cluster of grass houses. Not a person was to be seen. I sat down outside the big hut where the kahuna had lived, and waited while the boy went to see if he could find someone.

I heard him shouting for a time and then it was quiet for several minutes. Pretty soon he came back with news. On the night I had sent back the death prayer to the kahuna he had been asleep. He had awakened with a scream and rushed around to get *ti* spirits. Between gasps he told the people what had happened. He had neglected to *kala* himself and the white kahuna had taken a low advantage of him. In a very short time he had fallen to the ground and lay there groaning and frothing at the mouth. He was dead by morning.

The people were certain that I had come to wipe out the entire village. I told the boy to go back and tell them that I had taken my revenge and that if they behaved themselves, I would consider them my friends.

We waited some time before the head man came back with his flock. He wasn't at all happy, and most of the women were frightened nearly to death. However, I soon reassured them, and in no time we were all great friends. In fact, they seemed to consider me quite a fellow. No one seemed to resent my having killed their kahuna—that was all a part of the game to them.

Some of the horses were tired out, so we accepted an invitation to stay and be feted. They gave us a *luau* (feast), which, considering the poverty of the village, was not bad. They had no pigs, but the dog was as tasty as you please—being *poi*-fed meat. I had never taken kindly to dog, but as a full-fledged kahuna, I no longer hesitated. We parted blood brothers.

The only thing which I could never understand about the matter is this: The old kahuna had found out that I had hired the boy—and by psychic means—but he had not found out that I had turned kahuna and was sending his death prayer back to him. The only way I can account for this is that he must have turned in for the night at dusk and gone at once to sleep.

Another thing which seems certain is that the kahuna was of a fairly powerful class. Only those well up in their art can see at a distance. Just why he had not seen into the future, I cannot say, unless he was not quite up to that.

8

How the Kahunas Foresaw the Future

Man has always been fascinated with the future. He anticipates it with fear or with eagerness; he either avoids it or tries to predict it. The Hawaiians share this fascination, and their lore is replete with the many ways in which they dealt with the future, according to their conceptual beliefs of the structure of the future.

The most essential belief held by the kahunas was that the future was not irrevocable. The future could be changed, they believed, and frequently it was. These changes were possible due to the way in which the priests understood the formation of the future.

According to Huna, it is the High Self that constructs the future out of the thoughts and the imaginings of the middle self. This jumble of conflicting desires and fears is relayed to the High Self via the low self, most frequently during sleep. The High Self then takes these thoughts—formed of *aka* substance—and fashions them into a very real future. Just as the physical body fits the mold of High Self's shadowy body, so do events and people fit this future mold created by the High Self.

Sleep is the most common time for thought forms to travel up the *aka* cord to the High Self, for in sleep, conscious barriers are lowered and the suggestible subconscious is more easily reached. Anyone desiring to actively influence the thought forms chosen by the High Self to be used in forming the future should begin his work with the sleep state.

The subconscious self is extremely suggestible. It is also incapable of any other than very rudimentary powers of reasoning. If a thought can be lodged in it, the subconscious will be persuaded to hand the thought form over to the High Self. In the case of planning for the future, thoughts lodged in the low self will be the ones used by the High Self to build a corresponding future.

One method of influencing the future, then, is to implant thought forms in the low self when it is asleep, its most suggestible period. This can be done with tape recorders set to play the desired message to the low self. If a tape recorder is used on a regular basis, the individual will adjust to the disturbance and cease to wake up when the message is played. The advantage of this method is that the message is being relayed to the low self at the time when contact with the High Self is most efficient.

Another method is the obvious approach through dreams. Precognitive dreaming is common to a great number of people and can easily be developed by others. The only major stumbling block to precognitive dreaming is the dreamer's inability to remember his dreams. Once the knack of remembering is acquired, one will be surprised to learn that precognition is not an art that must be studiously learned, but a natural occurrence. As all psychic experiences (according to kahuna lore) come from the low self and sleep is the state most conducive to psychism, the low self, during sleep, has greater freedom to cognize the future and manifest its cognition through the element of the dream.

Precognition in dreams can manifest as symbols, which need to be interpreted, or as actual visions, which need no interpretation. The use of symbology is far more common in dreams; therefore, the individual who is able to remember his dreams is urged to keep a dream notebook and to try to decipher the symbols for precognitive flashes.

For those who cannot remember their dreams, here is an easy way to train oneself to do so:

1. Just before falling asleep instruct the low self to remember all dreams. Give it the suggestion to wake you up each time you have dreamed.

2. Have paper and pen by your bedside, ready to record your dreams. This will also act as a physical stimulus to the low self, impressing it with the seriousness of your intent.

3. Each time you awaken, carefully record all your impressions, however fragmentary.

It is not unusual for one to take some time before he remembers his dreams in detail. The important thing is to record something each time upon awakening. If, at first, no impressions are recalled, record your mood. How did you feel when you awakened? You may very possibly carry the emotions you experienced in your dream into your immediate waking state.

As the technique is developed, it will become evident that dreams of the future are not primarily given to warnings of accidents, deaths, or other troubles. It is the normal, daily events that are seen for the most part, and symbols are most frequently used to relay this information. The vision of startling clarity is usually reserved for either changes or events of monumental import to the individual or to changes affecting the lives of many.

The kahunas gained their knowledge of the future through other psychic techniques in addition to dreaming. One of these additional means was the ancient art of "scrying," or crystal gazing. Crystal gazing produces a condition of relaxation in which the low self is able to enter a state similar to that of sleep, with the difference that the middle self is able to stand by and observe the dream-like images that appear in the crystal. Thus remembering is not a problem, but achieving a suitable state of relaxation is.

Max Freedom Long's investigation of both precognitive dreaming and crystal gazing led him to concede the advantage of crystal gazing over ordinary dreaming, however, due to the element of control in the former. When one gazes into the crystal, he decides what part of the future he wishes to see. When one relies on the dream method, he is forced to take whatever can be haphazardly intercepted.

In the West, psychical researchers seem to agree on five general types of precognitive experiences. At the most elementary level is subliminal precognition, or the "hunch" that proves to be an accurate one. Next comes trivial precognition, which takes place only a short time before the actual occurrence of a rather unimportant event. Then, in the area of full-blown, meaningful precognitions, which indicate a power of mind not limited by space or time, there are beneficial, nonbeneficial, and detrimental previsions.

In a beneficial premonition, the transcendent self may overdramatize a future event in such a way that it proves to be a warning which is acted upon by the conscious self's characteristic reaction to such a crisis.

To take an example from psychical researcher Louisa Rhine: A young mother in Washington State awakened her husband one night and related a horrible dream. She had seen the large ornamental chandelier that hung above their baby's crib crash down into the child's bed and crush the infant to death. In the dream, as they ran to discover the terrible accident, she noticed that the hands of the clock on the baby's dresser were at 4:35.

The man laughed at his wife's story, rolled over, and went back to sleep. Although she felt foolish for doing so, the young woman slid out of bed, went into the nursery, and returned with the baby. Placing the sleeping child gently between them, the woman fell at once into a deep sleep.

A few hours later, the young couple were awakened by a loud, crashing noise. The sound had come from the nursery, and the couple found that the chandelier had fallen into the baby's crib. The clock on the baby's dresser indicated the time as 4:35.

For the young woman's deep subconscious level, the falling of the chandelier was a *present* fact that was still a *future* fact for her conscious self. The absence of the baby in its crib was also a present fact to the transcendental self because it was aware of how the conscious self of the young woman would react if she knew the safety of her child was threatened. To stimulate the woman to action, the deep level of her psyche formulated a dramatic precognitive dream with an attached tragic ending. The future, therefore, had not been altered by the woman's action, only implemented.

Volume L, Number 3, of the *Journal* of the American Society for Psychical Research carries a fascinating account of statistical research conducted by William E. Cox, which seems to indicate that subconscious forewarnings (or "hunches") may keep people off accident-bound trains.

Cox selected passenger trains for his study for two basic reasons. First, the passenger-carrying capacities of airplanes, ships, and buses is fixed, while a train can add or remove cars as the traffic demands. Second, subways and buses do not keep the kind of accurate records of passenger traffic that would be required for such a narrow statistical study as the one Cox was about to conduct. To prove his hypothesis, Cox needed to obtain both the total number of passengers on the train at the time of the accident and the total number of passengers on the same train during each of the preceding seven days, and on the 14th, 21st, and 28th days before the accident.

Cox compiled separate statistics for Pullman passengers. He reasoned, quite logically it seems, that, as Pullman passengers had usually reserved their space on the train sometime in advance, they would be less likely to give credence to a subliminal precognitive or a hunch that they should not carry out plans made previously. Also, someone who has established a thought pattern of a business or pleasure trip and has been contemplating the activity for a number of days would probably have a mind that was hyperactive rather than in the relaxed state so conducive to "psi" phenomena.

The statistical tables compiled by Cox demonstrated the astonishing evidence that passengers did avoid accident-bound trains. In a study that concerned eleven train accidents, seven of the eleven carried fewer coach passengers than they had carried on the previous day; six carried fewer passengers than they had the same day on the preceding week, and four carried the lightest loads of the eight-day period.

In an investigation of seventeen accidents involving Pullman passengers, ten of the trains carried fewer passengers than they had on the same day of the previous week. Five carried the lightest load of the eight-day period. Cox later extended his research to include thirty-five accidents, and found that his data applied to eighty percent of the cases. With the final results of Cox's figures, the odds are better than 100 to 1 that some form of "psi" was involved rather than pure chance.

In 1934, H. F. Saltmarsh issued a report to the London Society for Psychical Research in which he had made a critical study of 349 cases of precognition. Saltmarsh established the following conditions which would, in his estimation, make a case of precognition wholly satisfactory:

1. It should have been recorded in writing or told to a witness or acted upon in some significant manner *before* the subsequent incident verified it.

2. It should contain a sufficient amount of detail verified by the event to make chance coincidence unlikely.

3. Conditions should be such that we can definitely rule out the following as explanations: telepathy and contemporary clairvoyance, autosuggestion, inference from subliminally acquired knowledge, and hyperesthesia.

Saltmarsh used these criteria to proclaim 183 of the 349 cases as being wholly satisfactory cases of precognition.

Saltmarsh theorized that what we call the "present moment" is not a point of time, but a small time interval called the "specious present." According to his theory, our subconscious minds have a much larger "specious present" than our conscious level of being. For the subconscious, all events would be "present." If, on occasion, some of this subconscious knowledge were to burst into the conscious, it would be interpreted as either a memory of a past event or a precognition of a future event. We know that the past is neatly catalogued somewhere in our subconscious. Some "psi" researchers, such as Saltmarsh, believe that all events—past, present, and future—are part of the "present" for the deeper transcendental mind.

In his book *An Experiment with Time*, J. W. Dunne gives many examples of his own precognitive dreams, which he recorded over a period of several years. Dunne firmly believed in sleep and dreams as the prime openers of the subconscious and formulated a philosophy, which he called "serialism," to account for precognition. In Dunne's view, time was an "Eternal Now." All events that have ever occurred, that exist now, or that ever will be, are everlastingly in existence. In man's ordinary, conscious, waking state, his view is only of the present. In sleep, however, the individual's view might be sufficiently enlarged to allow several glimpses of the future. Although Dunne's theory is considered too deterministic by the majority of "psi" researchers and has been generally discredited, the philosophy of "serialism," as advanced in *An Experiment with Time*, offers the challenge of bold and imaginative thinking.

One of Dunne's theories in relation to *deja vu*, the sense of the already seen, is quite intriguing. Dunne suggests that this curious experience (which almost everyone has had at one time or another) of "having been here before" is due to the stimulation of a partially remembered precognitive dream. When the conversation becomes familiar or the new location becomes suddenly recognizable, one may, according to Dunne, simply be remembering a precognitive dream, which has been driven back into the subconscious.

"Seeing into the future is contrary to present scientific beliefs," Long muses, "as are fire-walking and instant healing. Science has no explanation to offer and is stalemated on these points, but the kahunas show the way ahead for those of open mind who are ready to investigate the evidence which has been accumulated."

It is difficult to adjust to the Hawaiian concept of the future if one does not accept the phenomenon of precognition. But if one concedes that the future can be foreseen, it takes only an interesting stretch of the Western imagination to grasp the kahuna idea of a High Self with superior mental powers which enable it to see far ahead. Furthermore, argues Long, if the High Self used the type of reason that middle selves use, it could only guess at the future. And anyone connected with precognition can attest to the remarkable details expressed in predictions. Pure chance removes these detailed predictions from the realm of guessing.

"This means," Long insists, "that there is either a magnificently superior form of reasoning or super-reasoning brought into play, or as the kahunas believed, the future event or condition is actually a real thing, formed though it is of invisible shadowy body substance similar to that of which thought forms are composed."

The theory has intriguing implications. "If the High Selves," suggests Long, "working in a union or oneness quite beyond our comprehension, take the deeds and thoughts and desires of the world of middle and low self humanity, and, averaging all these, produce the pattern of the future, then that pattern is visible on the High Self plane of consciousness and set, insofar as the main pattern of the future is determined.

"The kahunas believed that the great events of the future were set and could be foreseen far ahead. World or national events might be seen hundreds or even thousands of years ahead. The future of the individual, because of the shortness of a human life span, could be seen only months or years ahead. The kahunas demonstrated their abilities to change the future of the individual, leading one to wonder about the possibility of enough force being gathered to change the future of the nations and the world."

The above statement will probably sound anathema to those believing in predestination, while striking the skeptics as wishful thinking. But the files of Huna researchers are filled with stories of unwanted futures being changed to the better by kahunas. The native Hawaiians made a practice of consulting a kahuna any time they could see their future heading toward rocky shoals, and there is startling evidence that they were successful in rerouting it.

Long has described in detail his own experience with changing an unwanted future. The year was 1932, and Long owned and operated a camera store in Hololulu. If one knows his history, he will remember that it was not an auspicious time for business. The Depression had hit Long's little camera store hard. Threatened with the loss of everything, Long went to a kahuna friend of his.

She was a woman, about fifty years old. After learning that Long was in trouble, she led him into her dining room and sat down at the table. While she smoked, she had Long explain his difficulties.

Long had decided that the only thing he could do would be to sell his business—including stock and fixtures—or go bankrupt. The only person in Honolulu who could have bought Long's store was his competitor, who owned a larger and older camera store.

Three times Long had gone to this man to try to get him to buy out Long at a very low figure, but each time he had failed to interest him. The lease on Long's store would run out in a few short weeks. To renew the lease for another five years with an advance in rent was out of the question. If the competitor did not buy, Long would lose everything.

After Long had explained all this to the kahuna and had answered a few questions, he was asked to think very hard and tell the healer exactly what he wanted to have come to pass. After reviewing the whole situation once more in his mind, Long announced that he wanted to sell his entire business to his competitor for eight thousand dollars. Even for depression times, Long felt that this figure offered the competitor a great bargain. In addition, Long expressed a desire to help his competitor amalgamate the two businesses, and after that, he wished to return to the Mainland and do some writing. He was quite definite.

Next the kahuna put several questions to Long, asking, "And if it happens that way, are you sure that it will not make a difference in your plans?" She explained that it was important that he not overlook any possible contingency and that he consider all the small details and imagine how each thing would react on some other part of the plan.

"The idea," Long explains, "was to make the 'prayer' to the High Self. The thought forms of the prayer had to be unmixed with doubts and uncertainties. They had to stand out clear and sharp and definite. An overlooked angle of the affair might bob up later to upset the working out of the plan."

The kahuna told Long that it had been her experience that most people sent to the High Self a continuous jumble of conflicting wishes, plans, fears, and hopes. Each day and hour they changed their minds about what they wished to do or have happen. As the High Self makes our futures from our averaged thoughts—which it usually picks up during sleep—our futures become a hit-and-miss jumble of contrary events, of accidents, and of good and bad luck. Accordingly, only the person who decides what he wants and holds to his decision doggedly, working always in one direction, can present to the High Self the proper thought forms from which to build his future as desired and planned and worked toward.

After this short sermonette and about an hour of discussion, the healer was satisfied. The next step, she announced, would be to contact the High Self and ask whether or not the plan was such that it could materialize.

The kahuna used a crystal-gazing technique of a smooth black stone swished with water in the bottom of a calabash bowl. She brought out a glass tumbler, filled it with water, grated half a teaspoonful of yellow ginger root into the water to cloud it and act as a physical stimulus to ward off spirit influence of the poltergeist variety, should any such be near. The grating, Long relates, was done with a thumbnail from a small piece of fresh ginger root out of the garden.

The healer asked for a silver dollar as a preliminary part of her fee. "This acted as a physical stimulus to her low self, as it represented a reward for work and service," Long explains. "This convinces the low self that it is a good thing for it to do."

The dollar was placed under the tumbler. The kahuna then shaded her eyes from the overhead light and sat for a short time looking down at the surface of the clouded water.

"Soon she began to see images and to get messages by some form of inner voice," describes Long. "She would remain in a trance-like state for a moment or two, rouse to speak to me to tell me what she saw, or to ask a fresh question. This continued for perhaps seven or eight minutes."

The visions in the crystal were all symbolic, and if the symbols were things she had learned by experience to know as good, she counted the answer favorable to Long's plans.

"She said she saw a door being opened," he remembers, "then a little later, a sheaf of wheat. She asked what these things might mean to me or if I had been thinking about them. She wished to be sure that she was not seeing them in my mind, but was instead truly receiving them from the High Self via the low self.

"When she was satisfied that the answer was favorable, she said, 'The god tells me that your prayer can be answered. The door is open. Your path is not badly blocked, even if the door was not open all the way. I will now ask what we must do for our part of the work.' "

Once more she gazed into the water and placed herself in a state conducive to receiving psychic impressions. She then began to see the competitor to whom Long wished to sell his business.

She described his appearance, checking with Long to determine whether she was seeing him accurately or not. By the time this psychic examination had been completed, the hour was growing late.

"Have you hurt anyone?" the kahuna asked. "Why is the door not wide open and why is your path a little blocked?"

Long could think of no injury done to anyone, and told her so.

"Do you feel that you would cheat your competitor if you sold your store for eight thousand dollars?"

Long assured the woman that he considered the deal most fair.

The healer sighed. "Then it is the little sin ideas which eat you inside because of your Sunday school or church training. Most of the good people, especially if they are good church people, have things like that. To get rid of the feeling of guilt and to clear your path to the god, you must fast until one o'clock for three days, and while you fast, you must not smoke. After three days, give a gift to some person in need or to some charity. This gift must be large enough to hurt a little—almost more than you can afford. This will make you feel deep inside you that you have done enough to balance all your little sins. After you have done these things, come to me again."

Long carried out the orders during the following three days, finding them difficult enough to impress his low self "not a little," he remembers. "I have been blessed with a good appetite and at that time I loved to smoke. My gift was made to the Salvation Army, this being to my mind a charitable organization."

Arriving in the evening of the third day, Long sat again with the kahuna at her dining-room table. Once more she made use of the tumbler mechanism, employing it in the same way as before. After a few moments she again saw the door, announcing that this time it was wide open. Now that the path was unblocked, she pushed away the tumbler and again closely questioned her client. Had he made any changes in his plans? Was he still sure that he wanted everything to happen just as he had stated?

When she had been assured that Long's plans were clear and unchanged, the kahuna prepared to make the prayer for him to the High Self.

"When a kahuna prayed to his or her High Self," interposes Long, "asking aid for a client, the prayer automatically went to the High Self of the client as well. This involves a belief that all High Selves are linked together in some way we cannot understand and can hardly imagine. They are 'many in one' and 'one in many.' They are unity in separation. They have bonds closer than those of bees in a hive. They have learned to work as a unit, but each does individual works."

To make the prayer, the healer rose and walked slowly back and forth, breathing heavily. After a few minutes she paused beside the table, quietly announced that she was ready to make the prayer, then, looking into the distance, she began to speak in Hawaiian. She spoke slowly, with great force, voicing the prayer once, repeating it, then repeating it once again.

"This thrice-spoken prayer was offered word for word and idea for idea as nearly as possible," relates Long, "the full force of the suggestive will being mustered to cause the low self to carry to the High Self the thought forms which were being made by the carefully and firmly repeated prayer.

"The High Self was contacted by the low self after a direct command from the middle self of the healer, the tumbler was not used, for this time no return answer was expected or requested. When the prayer had been thrice spoken the healer resumed her seat and took a cigarette. She smoked and rested after her effort. She had accumulated extra vital force and had presented the prayer as a set of thought forms on a flow of vital force."

Soon the kahuna brought the tumbler once more into play, this time to see what message could be had from the High Self, and what instructions might be given. As the water cleared, the healer saw Long doing several things. The old future had been torn down and a new one had been instantly reconstructed for him. The healer was now seeing the newly rebuilt future. She described to him the things she saw him doing and told him why he must do these things.

She saw him going to his competitor with a paper in his hand. On that paper he had written out his proposition to sell, his price, and all details. She said that the god had told her that this man was the kind who liked to see everything written down on paper, otherwise he would say "No" from force of habit.

"You write it all out," she instructed. "Then, next Tuesday, at a quarter after two, you go to see him. He will be in his office sitting at his desk and doing nothing. You put the paper on his desk and say, 'Have a look at those figures, will you? I'll be back in about ten minutes.' Then you go off, and in ten minutes, you come back. He will be finished reading your paper and will say to you that he will buy your business."

"At a quarter after two on the following Tuesday I went to my competitor's office with my proposal carefully typed out in full," Long recalls. "I found him, as had been foreseen, idly sitting at his desk. I placed the paper before him and asked him to look it over, saying I would be back in ten minutes.

"In ten minutes I returned, and he was waiting for me. 'I'll take you up,' he said. 'I'll give you my check for a hundred dollars to bind the bargain and you can make out the bill of sale.' "

"So," Long concludes, "with the help of the healer and the High Self, the deal was closed. The price stipulated in the prayer was paid me. I stayed on to get my business amalgamated with that of my friendly competitor. Then, with the deal all completed, I reported back to the kahuna, paying her all she would allow, which was little enough considering the great service she had rendered me."

In retrospect, Long has decided that the old future, before the intervention of the kahuna, would probably have contained all the business failures that had seemed so inevitable to him. As he had feared them, so would he have visualized them, worried about them, and thus created thought forms of failure.

"We can only guess that the thoughts we make into thought forms are used in some way in shaping the future," postulates the student of Hawaiian lore. "At least, the thought forms tell the High Self what we hope, fear, desire, and plan. It seems that our futures are made from these thought forms with all care being taken not to intrude on our free will. We must be allowed to exert free will, and unless we ask for help, it must not be given lest that free will be canceled."

"The Hawaiians conceived of the future as made of invisible material, but still containing all the events and conditions which would materialize from minute to minute and hour to hour and day to day for as far ahead as the invisible outline of the future is 'crystalized.' This leads us to suppose that the future is made like the shadowy bodies of the low and middle selves, and as are the thought forms. Perhaps thought forms are made to grow into events. But even though we cannot say for sure how it is done and why it is possible, we can and do know that the future is made in some such way, that it can be seen as far ahead as it has been made, and that it can be changed."

This story may serve as evidence that—at least in one individual's life—the future was changed. Certainly it cannot be used as blanket proof that everyone's future might be altered, but it at least introduces the possibility.

Long's experience also points out some of the obstructions in the path of one who wishes to change his future.

The kahuna inquired of Long whether or not he had hurt anyone. The resultant formation of a guilt complex in the low self could provide the backdrop for a scene in which the low self refuses to contact the High Self, thus making a change of the future impossible. This is a familiar obstruction. Next the kahuna made sure that Long considered his proposed change ethical to all whom it would involve, and therein is the proverbial rub. The High Self will not undertake to do anything that would cause another to be hurt.

The High Self cannot interfere if the middle self creates thought forms of destruction of property or ill towards others. It cannot violate the entity's free will, which would be the kahunas' explanation for the chaos and insensitivity to others extant in the world. The High Self must be asked before it can render assistance, and the path must be unblocked. Then, if it is asked to correct injustice, it will comply. If it is asked to perpetrate injustice, it will refuse.

Let us recall the Hawaiian concept of union between all High Selves. The unit responds as a whole, but is capable also of responding to a part. It is both universal and individual. Therefore, if the High Self of one individual can effect changes in that person's life, what could the collective High Selves accomplish in the way of changes affecting the entire world?

"The kahunas demonstrated constantly their ability to foresee the future of the individual and to gain the aid of the High Self to change it for the better," Long states. "From this I believe we can conclude that the future of the world and nations might also be foreseen and changed by concerted effort, were we sufficiently enlightened. Today, when we consider the possible use of the atom bomb as a weapon, or the hydrogen or the cobalt bomb, we might, if greed did not rule the world, still be able to take such concerted action as to change what appears—even to our blind eyes—to be inevitable disaster.

"The kahunas taught that there was an ideal condition to which the individual might aspire. It was a condition in which the aid and guidance of the High Self was requested, received, and then acted upon. The one rule of life that must be obeyed is that we should do nothing to hurt one another. For those more advanced, the rule included loving service. Love can unite men and enable them to do great works for the good of all. Hate and fear can unite men only for war and destruction."

By way of comparison and, allowing for semantical differences, by way of demonstrating a certain psychic unity between the South Seas and the West, we might do well to close this discussion of how the kahunas foresaw and changed the future with the astute observations of the late British seer John Pendragon on the mechanics of how he was able to obtain his impressive and well-documented glimpses of the future:

> Most people seem to imagine that events that lie in what we term the future are "fixed" on a sort of moving belt that we call time, and that time moves the event out of the future into the so-called present and later into the so-called past. If they reflected for a moment, they would realize there is no such thing as the present. Utter the word "present" or "now," and even as you utter it, part of the word has vanished into the past, while the part yet to be uttered is still a fraction of a second in the future. Nobody can isolate a point in time and say, "This is the present." It is rather like trying to define a point or a line as Euclid did—it isn't there.
>
> It clearly seems, then, that time has something to do with consciousness. Either an event has not happened yet or it has happened—at least that is how it seems while we are apparently naturally and normally "locked" in our bodies, never forgetting that man is *not* his body. Man's body is only a building that he is living in for a few score years.
>
> If there is no present, how then is it that events are spaced out? If there is no present, then events must be either in the future or in the

past. "Now" seems a very real thing to us. Nevertheless, even this illusive now has something queer about it. Sometimes now seems much longer than other times. The passage of time is strangely elastic from the mind standpoint.

It is difficult even to attempt to conjecture on the nature of time, because one lacks an apt phraseology. Let me attempt to give my personal description, and please bear in mind that I am not an authority on the matter, in spite of the fact that I can see events before they happen.

Let us suppose that one has a very long table, and at intervals of two or three inches a small object has been placed. First, for example, a button, then a matchbook, a pin, a bead, and so on, until 50 or more objects have been spaced out down the table. Now the room is plunged into darkness.

A person who has no knowledge of the objects on the table enters the darkened room. (In effect, he is born.) He is handed a very tiny, low-powered flashlight with a beam sufficient to illuminate only *one object at a time.* He directs the beam on the first object—the button. The beam of light represents his consciousness. For a second, he recognizes and appreciates the object that he has illuminated. Then he moves the beam on to the second object, and at the same time, the first one "vanishes" into darkness again. Object one, by "vanishing," has moved into the past. Meanwhile, object two, being illuminated, is in the present, whereas object three and all subsequent objects are in the future. Finally, after he has illuminated each object in turn, he reaches the last one, and his illumination—his consciousness in a "beam sense"—goes out. (The moment of physical death.) Then somebody enters the room and switches on a big light over the table, and the examiner discovers that he can see *all* the objects at the same time. In short, his tiny beam of consciousness has been exchanged for a greatly enlarged one.

Now that we have reached this inadequate comparison, we might add that a clairvoyant has a second tiny lamp which he can direct upon objects far down the line. The non-clairvoyant (if I may coin a word), on the other hand, has to direct his little beam on each object in strict rotation. No such limitation is imposed upon the clairvoyant, who can direct his second beam backwards and forwards.

I may be wrong, but long experience has shown me—or appears to show me—that the stuff (I cannot find a more apt word) of the future is plastic. It can be molded by thought. In short, it is *psychoplastic.*

If we hold a mind-picture for a long time, we tend to materialize it, especially if there is no doubt in our hearts and if we do not alter that picture. If we alter the picture or begin to doubt, we cannot bring what we desire out of the immaterial to the material. It is rather like getting a jelly to set. One must not stir it. The more powerful the thought and the sharper the picture, the more quickly we shall be able to materialize it. Let me add that this technique is indeed a two-edged weapon, for it will work for both good and evil. In the latter, it is a case of "the thing I feared most has come upon me." The late Dr. Alexander Cannon, author of many works on the occult, told of a patient who was fearful of dying of a certain rare disease. She read everything that had been written about it, and daily dwelt upon her fear. In due time, she contracted the disease. *She had clothed her thought in matter,* but negatively so.

Thus it would seem that, to revert to the analogy of the moving belt called time, it is possible to determine by voluntary action what sort of thing is to reach us on the belt. But we have to bear in mind that not one person in ten thousand makes a *deliberate technique* out of getting what they want. Life to them is mostly a variegated patchwork of events. These persons are easier for the clairvoyant to "read." The less intellectual the subject is, the easier it is for the seer to determine his or her future. Complex minds are much harder to delineate. It is often hard for the clairvoyant to determine the difference between the subject's thoughts at a given moment and an event which stands in the so-called future. Since in my opinion it is also possible to mold one's future by deliberate thought (though I grant there may be limits to this, as I hope to show in a minute), it may be possible to change the nature of what the clairvoyant states lies in the future. In this case, the clairvoyant turns out to be "wrong."

To put it another way, in certain instances it is possible to change the nature of what is seen by the clairvoyant, but only by deliberate action. I recall reading of a case recently in which a woman dreamed she was in a car that had a tire blowout at a certain point on a cliff road. In the dream, the car plunged over the cliff. The day came when she was traveling in the car towards that point, but as the car neared the place where she had dreamed it would plunge over the cliff, the driver was ordered to slow down to three miles an hour. It was then that the car had the blowout—without falling to disaster over the cliff. Thus, it seems that what the clairvoyant "sees" as a "future event" may not necessarily be one, but the prediction is heeded and considered as a warning.

Let us take my warning letter to President Kennedy. Had he seen it and heeded the warning, he might be alive this day, unless he was *fated* to die at that time.

That last sentence is all-important. It brings me to the nature of fate. My own opinion is that fate operates rather like this:

A man may be fated to go from New York to San Francisco. This he is *fated to do.* There is no escape. He cannot go to any other destination. He must go to San Francisco.

The element of free will enters into the matter with regard to the mode and route of his journey. He can fly directly from New York, or he can go by rail or by road. If he chooses road, he can go by car or even by bicycle or on foot. He can go by sea, via the Panama Canal. He can go north and then west via Canada and then south again, or he can sail due eastwards and approach San Francisco from the west. In the selection of a route he has choice, but in one thing he has no choice—his destination. I think that in one or two things we are fated, but that in a vast number we have free will. Whatever route we decide to choose, however, we only choose it as another means of getting to our fated destination.

I have noticed, also, that those persons who govern nations are rather more fated than others. The same seems to apply to those whose life is involved with the guidance or service of large numbers of other persons. Occultists always seem notoriously fated.

I am deeply conscious that there are many possible answers to the age-old problem of fate and free will. I feel that it is always necessary to keep one's mind open. Anything in the nature of dogma must be avoided.

9

How Huna Regarded
the Question of Sin

According to Max Freedom Long, the ancient kahunas knew what the modern psychoanalysts have overlooked to a painful extent.

"When a man has 'sinned' and his low and middle self agree that he has sinned, the low self may have a fixed idea that punishment must be given for sin," Long comments. "If this is the case, the low self may set about punishing the man through illness or accidents."

Long is convinced of the urgency of the need for better understanding of the single and dual complex and the ways to combat them.

"Unfortunately, the present methods of treatment are far inferior to those formerly used by the kahunas," he says. "The most effective method is 'deep analysis' but this takes months of time and mints of money. If a cursory review of the case and a small amount of treatment by suggestion does not bring a cure, the patient has an alarming chance of joining those throngs which crowd the hospitals for the insane."

"A complex of simple nature or a dual one shared by both selves, if not allowed to have its way, creates a 'house divided against itself' which certainly will fall into insanity or chronic invalidism."

The kahunas had a very simple way of determining what was sin and what was not. One asked oneself whether any act was such that it injured another or hurt another's feelings. If the act hurt no one in any way, that act was not a sin.

The Huna system taught that God was too high and too all-powered for any human being to hurt by any mortal act.

"I cannot sin against God. I am too small," the kahuna would answer an orthodox Christian missionary attempting to convince the native Hawaiians of their sins against God.

"The sex urges are the most prolific sources of complexed ideas of sin with which we have to contend, since as children we are taught modesty and are shamed or punished for any display of sex interest," Long says. "Religious instruction implants the idea that sex urges are sinful and that, therefore, children are born from, and in, sin."

Dr. Brigham and Max Freedom Long found the kahunas to be logical in their approach to sex. If sex acts did not hurt another, they were not considered sins. In any case, such acts were not sins against Higher Beings. Sins were only acts that hurt other mortals.

In complexes built upon sexual restraints, the kahunas found that the low self may translate the externals of the complex several times. The result of such action may evade a long psychoanalytical study and fail to bring to light the original complex so that it can be talked over and submitted to therapy and brought under the control of the middle self, as are normal thoughts and ideas.

Sigmund Freud, Western discoverer of the subconscious or low self, decided that all complexes were based on sexual frustrations. Later psychologists have modified the severity of this decision, but there is still a school of psychology that holds with Freud and presents very convincing arguments to support his stand.

"Because the complexed low self will refuse to accept a suggestion to remove the symptoms of trouble caused by the complex, the healing value of suggestion is greatly lessened," Long explains. "Low selves refuse to accept any suggestion that is contrary to the subject's moral beliefs."

"Because the low self creates all of the emotions for us, it is possible in many instances to discover the presence of a complex or a fixation by watching for an emotional reaction when such a complex is stirred into action.

"We are accustomed to the spectacle of someone 'flying into a blind rage' over some trivial happening," Long illustrated. "It may only be a word that touches off an emotional explosion, but once that trigger has been touched, the full force of all former rages connected with the circumstance that created the complex in the first place is released."

Although modern psychoanalysts have never found a simple and effective method of finding the complex and bringing it to light to be rationalized and drained off, Max Freedom Long claims that there is a procedure to be learned from the Huna system.

"This method is a violent one," Long cautions. "It will seem very strange to the civilized man at first glance, but no stranger than the use of violent insulin shock on insane patients in modern asylums.

"We must recall the fact that the Huna system held that thoughts were invisible little things (thought forms) and that they were very real and substantial. The thought form, *aka* is made when we think. Every thought is made into a permanent thought form which joins others in clusters of associated thoughts, thus linking one thought to the one which came before or after it, and to all similar thoughts.

"We must recall, also, that the thought clusters flow on currents of vital force, which in turn flow along tiny threads of shadowy body material connecting two persons. When a kahuna and any practitioner of healing gives a suggestion, there is a flow of vital force from him to the subject, both through hands placed upon the subject and through shadowy substance threads which connect the two after the first physical contact, or through contact established by the line of sight or the sound of the voice. One might also establish contact with another while traveling during sleep in the shadowy body or by employing the assistance of spirits of the dead.

"Suggestion is the implanting of a strong thought form in the low self of the subject," Long said with great emphasis.

"The 'will' or middle-self voltage of vital force is not the hypnotic agent. It only directs its own low self to plant the thought form of the suggestion in the shadowy body of the low self of the subject. The effectiveness of the suggestion depends on the acceptance of the thought form by the low self of the subject."

As has already been emphasized, in the Huna system, the acceptance of the thought form of a suggestion is greatly hastened by the use of a physical stimulus, i.e., something physically real that may be sensed by the low self of the subject and which will make it believe that a real something is behind the suggestion.

Max Freedom Long believes that the vital secret of dealing with a complex is to make the low self of the patient accept a suggestion contrary to its complex of belief.

"This is done by an almost violent use of low voltage vital force," he explains. "It is not necessary to search for the original complex of the patient through deep psychoanalysis. It is not necessary to study the patient's dreams for symbols and hints. No matter whether the original complex has been translated from one form to another and to another, it can be treated by suggestion.

"Remember the case of Dr. Brigham and the death prayer that was directed at one of his boys while in the mountains of Hawaii on a collecting expedition? The death prayer charged low self spirits with great volts of low *mana*, then sent them to contact the victim and discharge into him the full shock force of the charges. The shock force broke down the resistance of the victim's low self, and if he harbored a guilty thought or complex, it would have made the work of the low self spirits that much easier.

"The secret of forcing the low self of a patient to accept a thought form of suggestion lies in the use of an overpowering shock of a large charge of vital force to accompany the offering of the suggestion," Long said firmly.

"The importance of the kahuna methods of dealing with psychological complexes may be better grasped if we realize that in the United States alone we have hundreds of thousands of men and women needing psychiatric help. We have very few trained psychoanalysts to meet this need, and only a handful of them have learned to use suggestion to help delve for the complex. None know the method of shock with charges of vital force to cause the patient to accept suggestion to replace the complex."

10

The Kahuna Method of Instant Healing

Orthodox religions explain the miracle of healing by declaring that God or a saint or some other superhuman agency performed the act. Only the kahunas have offered detailed explanations of how such things are accomplished.

The kahuna theory of instant healing is one which involves (1) a High Self with a superior form of mentality and with ability to do the work; (2) the high voltage of vital force or *mana*, natural to all High Selves, and used in all miraculous works; and (3) the flesh, bone, and blood of the injured limb and the *aka* or shadowy body of the patient, particularly that part of it which duplicates the injured part of the body.

"The kahunas believed that the shadowy body of the low self is a mold of every cell of the body, also of its general shape," Max Freedom Long explains.

"To heal a broken bone, the High Self dissolved the injured bone and other tissues into ectoplasm, this usually being invisible, but not always. As the shadowy body mold is made of invisible (etheric?) substance, it cannot be broken or injured. Thus, with the mold of the normal leg there at hand, the ectoplasmic material of the dissolved parts is resolidified in the mold, with the result that the healing is instant and the limb is restored to its former condition."

Max Long is convinced that this explanation applies equally to all healing in which abnormal conditions of deformity or disease prevail. If there is a cancer, it is changed to ectoplasmic substance and then made into normal tissue to fill the mold of that part of the body as it was before the cancer developed.

"Although the kahuna explanation is relatively simple to state in general terms," Max Long cautions, "it must be noted that there are certain conditions which must be made right, if they exist, before healing is granted.

"There must be no complexed doubt or conviction of sin or guilt that has not been cleared away. What has been called 'faith' is a condition of freedom from any hindering complex."

One kahuna referred to the complex or fixation of ideas as the "thing eating inside." A conviction held by the low self may not be a correct belief, but once it is fixed in the memory of the low self, it is difficult to find and even more difficult to remove.

Max Long reminds us that modern psychology has explored the subconscious and found the complex, making it unnecessary to go to great lengths to prove that the kahunas were right in believing that such things exist and cause psychic difficulties.

"One thing, however, which modern psychology has not yet learned, but which the kahunas knew to their profit, is the fact that all efforts to remove a complex will be far more successful if those efforts include a combination of logical appeal to the patient's conscious self, mild suggestion, and the use of a physical stimulus to accompany the administering of suggestion," Max Long points out.

"The low self is so accustomed to having the middle self think of imaginary things, that anything resembling an imagining is paid scant attention," he continues.

"The low self is best impressed by real and tangible things. For instance, the water used in religious ceremonies to 'wash away sins' is something tangible, and therefore impressive to the low self. Kahunas have used water in the ceremonial cleansing of the patient while giving the spoken suggestion that all sins are being washed away. They have used many other physical stimuli for, perhaps, ten thousand years."

Actual proof that broken bones can be dissolved into invisible etheric substance or ectoplasm, then made solid again as bone in the unbroken mold of the shadowy body, is difficult to establish, because nothing is to be seen by the observer. In the annals of psychical research, however, we find accounts of visible and tangible bodily tissues and other substances which have been seen to vanish into nothingness and to reappear via processes known as "dematerialization" and "materialization."

While the kahunas were unable to give a detailed explanation of how the High Self used the high voltage of the vital force to control dematerialization and materialization, they were very certain that this force was used and that it was nearly always provided by the living flesh. The kahunas were also certain that the shadowy body was always an important part of the process.

11

The Life-Giving
Secrets of Lomilomi

According to the semihistorical legends of the South Seas, the healers of Hawaii often made use of *lomilomi*, physical manipulation, as an aid to what might be termed "mental" healing.

"If we modern people would combine Swedish massage, the various baths, chiropractic, osteopathy, the use of suggestion, and the ancient religious practice of the 'laying on of hands' to heal, we should approach the scope of *lomilomi* as a skilled kahuna might practice it," Max Freedom Long has said.

The first step, the use of thermal baths, is familiar to all races. As Max Long has reconstructed the *lomilomi* procedure, the herbal decoction of the Hawaiians was frequently made with the leaves of the *ti* plant and held a supposed power to drive away any spirit of the low self class that might be trying to steal vital force from a patient. Natural mineral springs that provide hot water for baths, including hot mud, are known to give relief in many kinds of illness. The Turkish or hot steam bath is a substitute, and among the Navaho and other Indian tribes prolonged steam baths were taken as a means of purification before certain ceremonial rites.

"The application of heat, through stones or other mechanisms, has been used by healers for centuries," observes Long. "Modern doctors apply heat in various forms, deep electrical, surface, lights and so on. If there is to be a manipulation of joints, heat is used to relax tense muscles and allow easier movement."

The second step of *lomilomi* involves the manipulation of joints, deep massage, and rubbing to increase the patient's circulation.

"While it is certain that the natives who practiced deep massage after heating and relaxing the muscles did not have a clear understanding that certain spinal joints might be slightly slipped and pressing on nerves, as has been demonstrated by osteopaths and chiropractors and has been denied by orthodox medical doctors, the kahunas did an excellent job of making adjustments," Max Long states. "They pressed or pulled or twisted until a joint 'popped,' if they were able to make it do so. Most joints when so manipulated fall back into their proper alignment if the displacement has not been of too long standing. After the use of heat for relaxation and deep massage and rubbing to increase circulation, the patient was allowed a period of rest—an excellent thing in itself."

The third step in *lomilomi* is one that we moderns have still to learn. This step involved the use of the vital force in healing.

"The nearest we have come to it is the application of electrical currents of varying kinds through the use of electrical machines," Max Freedom Long comments.

"It is agreed in some medical circles that the electrovital force of the body must be up to a certain strength to maintain health. Scientists have successfully measured body waves and brain waves and some progress has been made in the study of their significance in the bodily and mental health and illness."

According to the studies of Dr. William Tufts Brigham and Max Freedom Long, knowledge of the vital forces and mild forms of hypnotic suggestion went hand in hand in the kahuna practices of healing.

"In the West, we made a good beginning toward recovering the ancient Huna practice of giving the patient vital force while administering the suggestion of healing with the discovery of mesmerism," Long observes. "Mesmer, who demonstrated the power of suggestion over a century ago, believed that he was healing by transferring to the patient some of his own 'animal magnetism,' and that this force did the healing."

Max Long believes that what Mesmer and his followers actually did was to use the transfer of vital force as a healing agent, coupling it (unknowingly) with the use of very potent suggestion. Dr. Braid, who lived much later than Mesmer, discovered the fact that hypnotic suggestion could be given and made to take effect without physical contact between patient and operator.

"Dr. Braid gave the world a knowledge of hypnotic suggestion," Max Long notes, "but he caused the almost utter loss of the fact that vital force could be made to flow from one person into another with beneficial healing effects. The doctors who use suggestion in healing and as an adjunct to psychoanalysis and the draining off of fixations are still lacking a definite and very important part of their healing art."

Long believes that the simplest application of treatment with shared force is the act of the "laying on of hands." When the healer "lays on hands" and prays to God to bring about healing, miraculous cures can be wrought if the High Self has been contacted and acts. Otherwise, the best that can be expected is that the desire to heal will act as a hypnotic suggestion to cause the vital force of the healer to enter the patient and take with it the suggestion of health.

> Vital force—bodily electricity or low *mana* (the voltage peculiar to the low self and the body, not the middle self and the will or mind)—has an amazing characteristic which is still unknown to modern researchers (Long emphasizes).

> This characteristic is that the *mana* responds to the commands and direction of the consciousness of sentient beings almost as if it were itself conscious!

> The kahunas have passed down to us in a vague and tangled form the information that the universe has been created by the action of consciousness upon force to create matter. Science tells us that all matter is made up of an electrical form of force or energy which has been set to moving in certain relations to other units of moving force, and that—seemingly because of the balance between the positive and negative forces in any given combination—we have the various forms of matter.

> Huna tells us that the thing which sets this electrical force into fixed motion is consciousness. The High Self can use its consciousness to cause vital force to become high in voltage and to cause changes in temperature and matter—as in fire-walking and instant healing.

> Above the level of the High Self are supposed to be still higher levels of consciousness which are entirely beyond human conception, but which create on a world scale. In Huna, one prays to the High Self, asking it to pray in turn to these still higher Beings if such prayer is required. Such a procedure is somewhat akin to the Christian practice of praying to God through the meditation of Jesus, the Son of God.

> The important thing to be learned from the kahunas is the fact that when vital force flows from one person to another, it may carry

with it various substances, particularly *thought forms*, or thoughts embodied in their tiny shadowy bodies.

This secret of the kahunas throws a new light on suggestion—auto suggestion as well as hypnotic suggestion. The art of suggestion consists of transferring to someone else some of your low *mana* or vital force and, on the flow, sending the thought forms of the suggestion—be it one of health or of actions to be taken by the recipient of the suggestion.

In giving suggestion the contact may be made by laying the hands on the patient. However, if the patient has once been touched, a thread of shadowy body material thereafter connects the healer to the patient, and when a "willed" command is given to the low self of the healer to reach out along the thread and touch the patient, even at a distance, contact can be made and vital force and the thought forms of suggestion sent, as along a telegraph wire. This is "absent treatment," or treatment by telepathic means. To use this form of treatment takes training and practice.

Max Freedom Long states that a further secret of great importance was the kahunas' knowledge that if a physical stimulus was used to accompany mild suggestion, the effect would be enhanced to a marvelous degree. "A physical stimulus is a material something, or act, which impresses the low self of the patient," he explains.

Lomilomi is at its best when it includes a suggestion given at the time that vital force is transferred through the hands of the healer, and the massage and manipulations act as a physical stimulus. Medicine might be administered as an additional physical stimulus, as well as herbal baths and doses.

These are life-giving secrets indeed (Long maintains). Vital force, *mana*, is life. Without it, consciousness in the form of the low and middle selves cannot function. Without it, the physical body dies.

Restore the vital force and implant suggestion in the mind of the low self that the force is to be used for healing the body. Use a physical stimulus to cause this suggestion to be accepted. Do this while laying on hands, or use absent treatment through the connecting threads of shadowy body material. This is low magic, while prayer to the High Self and instant healing is High Magic.

12

The Horrid Things of Darkness

Max Freedom Long warns:

> There are horrid things which belong in the realm of darkness, but which we are powerless to combat because we have become too civilized to realize that they are there. Doctors know nothing of them. Priests and ministers have such a garbled idea of devils that their advice is useless. Spiritualism knows only enough to be afraid, to warn dabblers to be careful.
>
> Modern occultists have guessed at a whole plethora of evil things and have written gravely about "black" magic, spells, and enchantments. They draw their magic circles and retreat within them to escape the dark forces, not sure that such forces are present. They hark back to the Middle Ages and employ the talisman and the charm.
>
> The practitioners of mental healing recognized these forces as "malicious animal magnetism," little understanding their nature, but waging frequent war on them when their activities were suspected.
>
> All primitive people know something of them, but their methods of meeting the threats of the dark ones are of precarious value.
>
> Among the priceless gifts which the kahunas have given to the world is a clear and comprehensive knowledge of the horrid things of darkness and an effective way of fighting them.
>
> It is vitally important that we gain the right understanding of things here, for when we die and cross into the after-life in the shadowy bodies, the things we have believed here become almost fixations, and may haunt us there.

Long believes that when any sentient being dies and takes up life in the invisible world in its shadowy body, it makes its own level or gravitates to it through its thinking. If the shadowy body thinks of familiar surroundings on earth, it makes such surroundings in the afterlife. The kahunas say that the spirit makes everything out of the shadowy stuff of dreams. Through these dream scenes and places, however, move real and genuine spirit beings. Thus, a man when he dies enters a world of dream scenery, sharing the dream scenes of his friends and relatives and adding his own touches.

Psychical researchers have determined that the spirits of the dead seldom, when in contact with the living, report that they have gone to a place unlike the earthly places to which they were accustomed. The spirits find themselves clothed as they were on the earth plane, and they live in similar houses; the spirits of certain Eskimo tribes report living in the same lands of ice and snow as they did on this side. The dead who expect to arrive in a Christian heaven report finding one. Those who imagine purgatorial scenes find them.

"Hell alone seems not to be peopled," Max Long observes, "perhaps because no one really expects to be judged utterly bad."

When Fred Archer, a former editor of the Spiritualist publication *Psychic News*, discussed the concept of afterlife with Canon Harold Anson, he found that the orthodox clergyman's view was remarkably similar to that of the Spiritualists. Canon Anson said that he thought that the soul would find itself in a world that would be in harmony with its own ideals.

"The real hell," the clergyman said, "will be to live in a purely carnal world until it becomes a perpetual torment, and the soul realizes its infinite mistakes. I am not shocked at Sir Oliver Lodge describing in *Raymond* the drinking of whiskey and smoking of cigars in the next world. After all," the canon continued, "Jesus says He will drink wine with His disciples."

In Volume 5, Number 1, of *Tomorrow*, H. H. Price, a former president of the Society for Psychical Research, London, puts forth the view that the whole point of our life on earth might be to provide us with a stockpile of memories out of which we might construct an image world at the time of our death.

Such a world, Price hastens to point out, would be a psychic world, not a physical one, even though it might seem a physical world to those experiencing it. The psychic world might, in fact, seem so tangible that the deceased, at first, might find it difficult to realize that he is dead. The causal laws which these image-objects would obey would not be the laws of physics, but laws more like those explored by Sigmud Freud and C. G. Jung. The incoherence of such a dream world of the disembodied would be incoherent only when judged by the nonapplicable laws of conventional physics, for the dream objects would not be physical objects.

Price theorizes that the other world "...would be the manifestation (in image form) of the memories and desires of its inhabitants, including their repressed or unconscious memories and desires. It might be every bit as detailed, as vivid, and as complex as this present perceptible world which we experience now. We may note that it might well contain a vivid and persistent image of one's own body. The surviving personality, according to this conception of survival, is in actual fact an immaterial entity. But if one habitually *thinks* of oneself as embodied (as one well might, at least for a considerable time), an image of one's own body might be as it were the persistent center of one's image world, much as the perceived physical body is the persistent center of one's perceptible world in this present life."

"There is a definite going on for those who know the afterlife conditions for what they are and who are thus enabled to escape being caught there and held back," Long says. "The goal is not that of reincarnation. Only a few come back to inhabit other bodies, as the Reincarnationists believe. The low selves come back as the middle selves of individuals being born on this physical level, but the middle selves, at least those from fairly civilized people, eventually go on to the level next higher. Those who know this secret waste little time in the 'summerland.' They obey the urge to evolve and to go on.

"The uninitiated," Long continues, "stay on for a very long time in the dream-surroundings, frequently coming back to contact the earth and loved ones here. Only now and then do they make trouble."

In the Huna view, the troublemakers are the low selves who get separated from their middle selves after death. They are the poltergeists that haunt houses and often molest the living. They are without the ability to reason, for they have lost contact with their middle selves and have become the spirits that obsess the living and sometimes render them insane.

The kahunas also believe that there are other low-self spirits who stay near the living by choice and who learn to touch the shadowy bodies of the living and steal vital force. If they can steal enough *mana* from the living, they can solidify their shadowy bodies sufficiently to enable them to move solid objects.

The kahunas hold that, for the most part, these low selves are fairly harmless, but they never lose sight of the fact that these low selves may become the horrid and darkly evil entities that stalk the living and prey upon them, stealing their vital force, often to the point of complete exhaustion and mysterious death, or of seizing their bodies and rendering them obsessionally insane.

"Thousands of the living are silently and invisibly haunted in this way, by low selves which appear as secondary or multiple personalities," Long states. "They are not 'split off' parts of the resident selves of a body, as is the popular belief today of our psychologists. They are individuals in their own right!

"Not only do the low selves, separated from their middle selves, fasten themselves on the living as parasite 'personalities,' but middle selves separated from their low selves do the same to a lesser degree, and now and again a normal ghostly spirit composed of both low and middle selves is guilty of taking up its abode in the shadowy body of a living victim.

"It is not for nothing that the living have an instinctive fear of ghosts," Max Long cautions us. "Dreadful things are done constantly to the living, with none to recognize the invisibles who are taking their life forces and, even worse, are implanting thought forms as suggestions into their low selves to cause endless erratic behavior, crimes, mischiefs, and sometimes utterly vile and evil acts."

The kahunas were also ever mindful of the danger of a purposeful attack by a spirit upon a living person in order to punish him for his acts against others in the flesh or to work revenge for acts perpetrated against the spirit when it was in flesh. The kahunas believed that the departed spirit could also use suggestion, especially if it could get a supply of *mana* from a living person and could acquire the thought form that had been used as the suggestion.

"A kahuna, in explaining this to me a long time ago in Hawaii, stressed the danger of thinking and voicing any thought which might be used as a suggestion by a normal ghost (a normal ghost is called *kino-wailua*, or body of two waters, water being the kahuna symbol of vital force. If a ghost had two kinds of vital force, it was composed of a low and middle self living in their interblended shadowy bodies)," Max Long recalled. "I was warned never to say, even in jest, 'He ought to be shot,' or 'I hope he chokes,' lest this thought be taken and given as a potent suggestion by some spirit enemy."

In Honolulu, Max Freedom Long studied a case of spirit attack involving the brother of a Chinese-Hawaiian friend of his. As Long tells it:

The young man had for a sweetheart a pretty Hawaiian girl. While he had not proposed to her, it was taken for granted that he would do so as soon as his financial affairs were in such condition that he could marry.

When his new business of salt making was established, his father stepped into the situation and demanded the customary right of the Chinese father to select a bride for his son. The son loved and respected his father and, although much embarrassed by his predicament, agreed to stop courting the Hawaiian girl and give time for a parental choice to be made. He knew that the Hawaiian girl would be deeply hurt when he broke off seeing her, but he was so filled with a sense of guilt and shame that he did not try to go to her and explain what had happened. Undoubtedly he developed a guilt complex which lodged in his low self and which was shared by the middle self in its conviction that he had done the girl a wrong.

The girl was heartbroken for a time, then fiercely angry at the treatment accorded her without a word of explanation. Following the tradition of her people, she began "grumbling," calling on the spirit of a beloved grandmother to avenge the wrong.

Soon the young man was overtaken by a strange malady. He would faint at unexpected times and without warning. He fainted and fell into a fire, burning himself painfully. He fainted while driving to his salt works and wrecked his car, narrowly escaping severe injury. He fainted and fell on his bed while smoking, setting fire to the bed and again burning himself. Three doctors were consulted, but none of them could diagnose the cause of the trouble. Almost from the first his Hawaiian mother had urged him to go to a kahuna, but the son was very modern and had been taught at school that the kahunas were superstitious imposters and nothing more.

When all treatment failed, however, he did as his mother suggested. The kahuna, then a man well advanced in years, listened to his story, sat for a time in silence with his eyes closed, then raised his head and announced that he had sensed the spirit of an old Hawaiian woman near him, and that from her he had learned that the young man had been guilty of one of the worst sins of all—that of hurting one who loved and trusted him. The spirit of the grandmother had been doing her best to avenge the injury.

The young man was amazed. He admitted his guilt and asked what he should do. The kahuna explained to him the ancient rule of the Hawaiians that no one should hurt another, bodily, or through theft of goods or through injury to feelings. These were the only sins, and for them there was but one remedy. The guilty one had to make amends and get the forgiveness of the injured party.

Taking his leave, the young man went directly to the girl. He was met by anger and disdain, but he persisted doggedly in his effort to make her understand his position in the matter. Scornfully she refused to be pacified. The next day he returned with gifts and more apologies, and the next day and the next. At last his pleas broke down the girl's anger and aroused her sympathy. She forgave him and agreed to go with him to the old kahuna to acknowledge her forgiveness.

The kahuna seemed to be expecting them. He praised the girl for her kindness, called to the spirit of the grandmother to observe that the wrong had been righted and forgiveness obtained. He thanked the spirit for having done so well in forcing justice to be done, and asked her to cease her attack. When she agreed to his request, he took a spray of *ti* leaves and sea water, sprinkled the girl and the air where the spirit stood, and spoke the words of the kala or forgiveness with suggestive power. Then dismissing the girl and the spirit, he turned to the young man, explaining that the *kala* (to bring back the "light") or cleansing for him was a more difficult matter.

Because he had been guilty and because his sense of guilt had made it possible for the spirit to place thoughts of fainting in his mind when she pleased, the punishment might even now be continued by his own low self (*unihipili*) unless it was well cleansed.

For the cleansing or forgiving ceremony he would have to use a very powerful and effective ritual—one which could not fail to cure the fainting forever. He brought an egg, holding it long in both hands and chanting a little as he commanded healing and forgiving power to enter the egg.

When the work of filling the egg with vital force was finished, he stood the young man before him and ordered him to hold his breath as long as he could. When he could hold it no longer, he was to put out his hand. In his hand would be placed a china cup into which the kahuna would have broken the raw egg while the breath was being held. Without drawing breath the young man was to gulp down the egg. At the same time the words of forgiveness would be spoken and, reinforced by the egg and the power in it, would effect the complete cleansing and cure.

The instructions were followed to the letter. The kahuna gave the suggestion of forgiving and of dispelling the guilt and fainting attacks. He continued the suggestions, rubbing the young man's stomach briskly after he had swallowed the egg and begun once more to breathe. The kahuna announced the complete success of the cure, warned the patient to forget the whole affair as soon as possible, and accepted graciously his fee for his work.

I investigated this case and checked all the details of the healing treatment. I also kept in touch with my young friend for several years following. Never once did the fainting attacks return.

13

How the Kahunas Treated Insanity

Western psychiatrists and psychoanalysts vary greatly in their attitudes toward psychical research. Those who profess nothing but an adamant skepticism contend that the alleged manifestations of paranormal phenomena brought forward by certain of their colleagues express nothing more than a desire on the part of those doctors to believe in the validity of ESP. But those who consider "psi" research to be a serious and valuable contribution to man's understanding of his own personality insist that paranormal activities, particularly those of telepathy and clairvoyance, are too numerous to be dismissed by an arched eyebrow or a cursory examination.

Many psychiatrists have developed a respect for "psi" research when, during the course of analysis, a close relationship that can only be described as psychic has developed between a doctor and his patient. Some doctors have reported patients who have related dreams that have dramatized actual incidents that the analysts themselves have experienced that day or even the week before. In several cases, the key to a patient's mental disturbance has been located in a dream experience of the analyst. Reports have even been made of several patients of the same analyst sharing dreams or reenacting group or individual experiences, as if some strange circle of telepathic dreams had been established.

Dr. Jule Eisenbud has said that the "psi" process should be used in analysis. "The psi process is a thorough-going part of the total behavior of the individual and as much of a determinant in the actions and thoughts of the patient as other types of stimuli."

Commenting on "psi" during therapy, Dr. S. David Kahn, a New York psychiatrist, has written that ESP can often bring to the surface material that patients and analysts have repressed.

Dr. Montague Ullman says that "many persons who are incapable of effective communication in normal ways can communicate at a telepathic level and surprise the therapist with a telepathic dream of rich awareness even of the physician's problems.

"The telepathic dreams reported by patients in analysis are at times striking and often ingeniously linked to the dynamics of the treatment situation. But the occurrence of the dream is episodic and uncontrollable. It appears under conditions in which no advance preparation is made to exclude sensory cues."

It would seem obvious that since so much of Freudian theory and practice has to do with the interpretation of the symbols created during the dream experience the bonds between psychology and parapsychology are strong indeed. The same ways of psychodynamics that apply to the dream also apply to "psi" phenomena. Both the dream and "psi" are incompatible with currently accepted notions of time, space, and causality.

Psychiatrist Dr. Jan Ehrenwald has theorized that at the lower level of the subconscious—which Freudian analysts refer to as the "id"—time and spatial relationships may be all mixed up. Here and there, past, present, and future may all be interlocked and interchangeable.

The problems that await teams of psychiatrists and parapsychologists working together in joint efforts are many and varied, but each question answered brings us that much closer to a unified picture of man's personality and his role in the universal scheme of things.

For example, what about the trance state? In what ways is it similar to, or distinguished from, normal sleep, religious ecstasy, or hypnotically or drug-induced states of unconsciousness?

What about mediumship? Does the medium serve as a receiving station for the unconscious patterns of others? Or is he in an altered state of personality, perhaps even possessed by a discarnate mind? And are the medium's spirit controls secondary personalities, or entities created by the mass mind of the seance circle?

And then, there is multiple personality with sometimes three, four, or five faces of some hapless "Eve." Could it be, as some researchers have boldly suggested, that the human psyche, in a parthenogenetic fashion similar to the division of cells, may give birth to another "self"? Could this literal "split" of the personality become dissociated from the original self and, scornful of the accepted dimensions of time and space, become a poltergeist?

Psychiatrists have assured us that the various "personalities" involved in extreme cases of multiple personality may operate independently of one another and may carry out activities exclusive of the conscious awareness of any of the other personalities. One personality may, in fact, perform a function which another "face" would be loathe to do under any circumstances. In such cases there are, for all practical purposes, two or more "people" living in one body.

The problems in "psi" research proliferate and desperately call for a united frontal attack by a strong alliance of psychiatrists, psychoanalysts, and parapsychologists.

In the Huna system, the treatment of the insane fell under two main headings: 1) the obsessionally insane; and 2) the insane whose brain tissues were injured, diseased, or abnormal.

Here, drawing upon years of research into the methods of the kahuna, Max Freedom Long explains how the Huna system dealt with the problems of insanity:

> If the brain is not normal at birth, the low spirit can function in the child but not the conscious or middle spirit. The low self cannot learn except as an animal learns. It remains unable even to use the low self's deductive reason, and so remains idiotic.
>
> The kahunas believed that the seat of the "mind" of the low self was in the shadowy body of the low self, and that this "mind" was in touch with a similar "mind" belonging to the middle self and seated in the shadowy body of the middle self. Both these minds usually keep in touch when the two spirits of a man leave the body during sleep or trance conditions. After death the two selves in their two interblended shadowy bodies leave the psysical body. Earth memories, beliefs, complexes, and ideas are stored in the shadowy body of the low self, so are taken along at death.
>
> Normally, the two selves use the body and its organs, the shadowy bodies penetrating and blending with all organic parts, including the brain, the nerve centers, and the nerves. If some of the brain centers or nerve tissues are lacking or become diseased, the selves cannot function through them. This is particularly true in cases in which the brain tissues used by the middle self are injured by sickness or

accident. The middle self, finding itself unable to function through its part of the body, becomes an outcast and leaves to wander about in the invisible levels. The low self, however, may be able to continue to live on in the uninjured parts of the body.

The asylums hold many insane persons of this class. The middle self is easily driven out of the body through a temporary or permanent injury to its nervous centers. Toxins from bad teeth or from disease may cause the middle self to leave, but the low self is able to function almost as usual. With teeth pulled or diseases treated, the middle self frequently resumes its residence in the body and sanity returns.

The low and middle selves may both be dislodged from the body by some abnormal condition or accident, and an obsessing spirit may take the body and hold it. Or the obsessing low spirit may gain possession of the body only at intervals, in which case the patient is said to suffer from "split personality."

In obsessional insanity the patient may be considered a victim of complete or reciprocal amnesia if the obsessing is done by a normal spirit made up of combined low and middle selves. When such a spirit drives out the rightful owner of the body and takes possession, it brings with it (stored in its own low shadowy body) the memories of another life in a body, and it brings also its own middle self and its characteristic reasoning powers. These cases are not typical of insanity because the obsessing pair of spirits is quite normal and sane.

Because the spirits who elect to remain close to some living person and steal a little vital force, if not able to steal the whole body, can often be called to enter the body and speak through hypnotic conditions, it has been thought that such spirits were split off parts of the original personality. When, through the repeated use of hypnotic suggestion, such obsession-bent personalities are forced to obey such suggestions as, "Unite with the main personality," there results a most amazing situation in which each patient is unlike any other. The main result is that the obsessing spirit, if a low entity and not a combined low-middle invader, can be brought under control of the resident middle self. This gradually results in the person having the memories of both low selves.

Modern treatment of the insane centers around the task of restoring normal health conditions if insanity has been brought on through illness or disease. In the ever-increasing percentage of obsessionally insane, classed by the doctors as sufferers from some form of "split off personality" or schizophrenia, the obsessing is done by a low self while the resident middle self is either driven from the body, or unable to control the invading low self. The characteristic thing in these cases is the loss of normal memories, showing that the original low self is displaced. There is another characteristic which points directly to a low self being involved. This is the tendency in this form of insanity to live in a dream or imaginary world, paying little or no heed to physical surroundings. Loved ones are not recognized except in the so-called "lucid" periods when the obsessing spirit may temporarily depart and the normal spirit return.

The treatment of hypnotic suggestion has long been regarded as a failure. The insane will not pay attention and seem to reject all hypnotic suggestion. This is natural for the reason that the low self or obsessing spirit has its own sets of beliefs and wishes, and suggestions contrary to these are rejected.

The insulin and electric-shock methods of driving out the obsessing spirit or spirits has been the most successful treatment yet discovered. If the pain produced by shock methods is sufficiently great, the obsessing spirit will leave, and—as it is not logical—it will be unable to understand the treatment and will conclude that the body will always be a painful place in which to reside. With the pain gone, the original spirits of the patient can return.

The kahuna method of treatment of the obsessionally insane made use of the shock method of dislodging obsessing low entities. The shock was produced by accumulating large quantities of vital force in the body of the healer and transferring it to that of the insane patient with the willed command that the invader be rendered helpless and thrown out of the stolen body.

The kahunas frequently used their psychic powers to sense the presence of the normal spirits of the patient and instruct them to stand by to take over the body once the invader had been put out. The help of the departed was also frequently asked for and obtained. A good normal person among the there-living (spirit world) could absorb large charges of vital force from the living and, thus greatly strengthened in will and in its shadowy bodies, could control the obsessing spirit once it had been put out of the body. Under control, it was often worked over to team it up with a middle self which had lost its companion low self—possibly the middle self with which it had formerly lived in a body before being separated in some way. (The rejoining of a low to a middle self in this way was a very good thing as it removed the danger of further obsessing activities on the part of the illogical and uncontrolled low self.)

The kahuna shock method, in which vital force is used as the shock-producing agent, has the advantage of forcing the obsessing low self to accept a thought form as a suggestion. The thought form here is that of withdrawing from the stolen body. Because of complex and related fixations held by the obsessing low self, the powerful suggestion was not always accepted and acted upon, although the theory was that, given a sufficiently large charge of shocking force, the suggestion would break down and replace all contrary thought forms held by the obsessing spirit.

While we have not yet taken up in detail the healing methods which involve the aid of the High Self, it may be said that it was believed that no human ill could be beyond the power of the High Self to heal. The High Self was especially able in handling obsessing low selves. The fact has been a part of religious knowledge the world around and for many centuries. When evil influences were sensed near or were suspected, the Christian crossed himself and prayed through Jesus to the Father. In India the rite took the form of intoning the sacred "Om," and in other parts of the world similar ritualistic appeals to Higher Beings were made. Charms and amulets were worn and were clutched while prayers for protection were made. While imagined dangers grew to outweigh by a thousandfold the real danger, the practice was basically sound in that a High Self was called upon for help and a physical stimulus was used in the form of the ritual crossing or intonation, holding of cross or amulet, etc., to cause the suppliant's low self to carry the prayer to his High Self.

Most of the low selves against whom protective measures need to be taken have fixed fears of the Higher Beings, these fears being carried as memories from their lives in the physical. If they were the low selves of a Christian man or woman, they would believe in God and Jesus, and when confronted with their dark deeds and a prayer and cross, would depart in fear.

It is highly probable that certain objects treasured in life by the living become fixation centers for them after death. (I have heard of many such cases.) It is also probable that when the living handle such objects they visualize with vital force the ancient threads of shadowy body stuff connecting the object to its former owner and attracting them to the living.

Such cases all stress the evidence which points to the fact that low selves on the other side of life are held over great periods of time by their fixed thoughts which have been carried across with them after physical death. If they have been separated from their logical middle selves, they cannot use reason to learn of their condition or to progress. They remain "earth bound," not understanding the significance of the change that death of the body has brought to them, and anxious to get back into a living body to continue the life they knew.

We, as civilized men, face another danger in that the insane are fed and housed, and only infrequently treated by insulin or other shock methods. This forms an open invitation to lingering horrid things out of the great past to obsess the living. It is not like it was in ancient days when "mad men" were stoned to death if violent, or left to starve after being driven out of the communities of the sane. This treatment was inhuman, but it was not an invitation to happy obsession in bodies which are fed, housed, and cared for in the modern way.

Of course, we will not return to cruelty in these matters, but we will come to a better understanding of the forces with which we have to deal, and learn more adequate methods of treating the insane.

From the foregoing it will be seen again how great a light is thrown on the dark places in our knowledge of ourselves by the lore of the kahunas.

14

Max Freedom Long Reveals Huna's Secret Within a Secret

This chapter has been compiled from excerpted portions of Max Freedom Long's *The Secret Science Behind Miracles*. Although slightly edited, the words, opinions, and arguments are those of Mr. Long.

The kahunas' secret within the larger secret was the fact that there was a third self connected with men and his two lower selves. The nature of this High Self (*Aumakua*) and the means of gaining its aid also belonged to the inner secret.

The kahunas knew that they could never do more than guess at the fact of, or nature of, Beings higher in the scale of consciousness than the High Selves.

They guessed that the Higher Beings would be similar to the lower ones they knew in man. They subscribed to the ancient axiom' "As above, so below." They may have originated it, for no other psycho-religionists seemed to have had definite and detailed knowledge of the three separate and independent spirits that comprise man.

The kahunas knew man to be a triune being—one of three spirits—so they guessed that the gods and even the final highest and Supreme Being would be triune in nature. This idea may have originated with the kahunas or it may not, but it spread around the world and appears in Christianity and Brahmanism, if not in the lore of the Great Spirit of the Amerindians.

Wherever the symbol of the triangle appears, it is safe to say that the secret of the triune nature of man, and possibly of the gods, was incorporated in the religion of the people. True, the real meaning of the three sides of the triangle representing the three selves of man may have been lost or misunderstood, but the symbol was retained and revered. In Egypt the pyramids presented to the world four faces of triangular form. In Central America the triangle was known and used in religion.

Another ancient and widespread belief common to the kahunas and later religionists was that there had been a descent into physical matter of some of the *consciousness of Higher Beings.* This accounted for the creation of the earth and lower forms of life and gave rise to various versions of the "Fall" which are found in several religions. As a logical result of a belief in a "Fall," there followed the belief that all lower creatures, headed by man, were on their way back up the scale, slowly returning to the Ultimate God.

Religions are filled with the intricacies of the descent and ascent, but because of his mental limitations, man of the middle-self level can never do more than speculate about them. The ways of the High Self are unfathomable in a large part, and the ways of still higher beings are totally unfathomable. The various scriptures, which are supposed to have been given mankind by divine revelation, portray the inventions of the middle-self mind. No two of the revealed writings agree. The only thing of which we can be fairly certain is that there is a High Self that can be approached for aid in the problems of daily living.

Some of the beliefs of the kahunas may be found in nearly all religions even if warped to uselessness and stretched to fantastic lengths.

The kahunas knew that the spirits of men come back at least once to be born again in physical bodies. The low self comes back to be born as a middle self in another human body. Some spirits may return to be born again several times in a physical body, but the idea of endless incarnations of man as a single spirit in innumerable bodies is an example of stretching an orignal idea to absurb lengths. In Christianity and in the teaching of the Jews, Mohammedans, and American Indians the idea of reincarnation is found only in vague reminders.

The same may be said in a way about the doctrine of Karma, which has become such a millstone around the necks of religionists in India. The original idea seems to have been that when we hurt others we lay ourselves open to spirit attack, or we form guilt complexes, and, because of them, are cut off from direct contact with our own High Selves.

The Hindu idea of Karma resulted from stretching the simple conception even more than the reincarnation idea. With some logic, it was taught that the "Law of Karma" began to function on the level of consciousness just below God-the-Unmanifest.

All beings lower than this Supreme Being had to be governed by the law. To complete the logic of this absurd guess at conditions on such unthinkable levels of consciousness, the "Lords of Karma" were invented to execute the fine justice. They had to have endless helpers to watch each sentient being in the lower heavens and on earth to record his good and bad deeds. The records had to be written, and the writing demanded a book, which was invented in the form of invisible *akasha*, where all records were kept and all things recorded to the last tick of time.

The Lords of Karma, as could be plainly seen, did not punish the wicked in the same incarnation in which the wickedness was perpetrated. The wicked flourished as the green bay tree. This flaw in the scheme was covered up by inventing the idea that punishment was administered in some later incarnation.

The same idea of an ideal and absolutely balanced divine form of justice is to be found in the Old Testament, but no attempt was made to cover with reincarnation the flaw of the flourishing wicked man. Punishment in hell was fully as effective and made a fine contrast with the idea of a heaven for the good after death.

In Christianity we find many ideas that did not come as a direct teaching of Jesus, and whose origins have been lost. The idea of the Lords of Karma is replaced by St. Peter as the keeper of the gate of Heaven and by the Book of Life in which, in some indefinite manner, the angel recorders keep an account of each life.

Christianity is the nearest to the original kahuna lore of any of the great religions. In the rituals of the Church of Rome—the origin of the rituals being unknown—we find the counterparts of the kahuna rituals used in healing.

The kahunas required a confession and used water that had been charged with vital force as a physical stimulus to accompany the spoken word of suggestion to "forgive" a patient or to break down a guilt complex after amends for hurts to others had been made. In the Roman Church, after confession, holy water is used in the ritual of forgiveness with the spoken words of forgiveness, but the part played by both complex and suggestion has long since been forgotten. The penance done at the order of the priest before the rite of absolution or forgiveness is, however, quite in line with the older rite as a good physical stimulus, even if there are sins to be forgiven which do not consist of hurt to others.

The kahuna methods of exorcising obsessing or haunting spirits is still to be seen in a way in the rites of exorcism of the Church.

The kahuna belief in the High Self or *Aumakua* is well preserved in Christianity. Jesus, according to the records as they appear in the New Testament, prayed to his Father in Heaven when he wished divine aid in performing miracles. That is what the kahunas did, only with a method of praying in which there was more ritualistic action because of the various elements involved.

In instructing his disciples, Jesus is reported as having said that they should also pray to the Divine Father, but stressed the fact that the prayer should be made in his name. This would be logical only if Jesus looked upon himself as a High Self. In any event, the matter is not one that will make the slightest difference in using a form of prayer to the High Self in obtaining aid in healing.

In India there is a hint in the *Bhagavad Gita* of the fact of the three spirits of man, but the High Self of the kahunas is confused with the "spirit of the Supreme," which is of an entirely different level. Because it is considered the duty of each person to suffer and so live down his bad Karma, no prayers are made by the majority of Hindus to gain aid from the Higher Beings in the matter of meeting the problems of daily life.

In Christianity there is a curious and almost unique mechanism to be seen in the vicarious atonement for sins. This doctrine is obscure in its origin, but closely resembles the kahuna belief that one can be forgiven for sins, instead of suffering under a hard and fast law of Karma to repay to the last iota.

Jesus made the final and complete atonement for the sins of the world by his death on the cross, according to Christian beliefs. These sins of the world seem to include the sins of the newly born babes who are "born in sin"—a strange dogma at best.

The Christian does not necessarily have to make restitution or amends in kind. In fact, he could not in case he had taken the name of God in vain, for his words could not be recalled. Logically, he would have to suffer in hell after death to make amends, but, according to the Christian plan of salvation, he may repent and get forgiveness from a priest or, better yet, by direct prayer appeal to God in the name of the great atoner, Jesus.

The kahunas, knowing that the Higher Beings cannot be injured by the living man and so cannot be sinned against, recognize no such sin as that of using profanity. The one recognized sin is to hurt a fellow human being. For such a hurt, amends must be made to the one hurt. In no other way can the evildoer convince himself that he has balanced his account and is no longer guilty, the guilt fixation held by his low self cannot be removed by the ritual cleansing (*kala*).

In the matter of forgiving the sin in Christianity and removing the guilt complex in the kahuna system, there is one point of great significance that must not be overlooked. It is the fact that the Christian believes that his sins are against God, as well as against man, and that he must receive forgiveness from God, even if not from those he has injured.

In kahuna practice, the Higher Being was not asked for forgiveness. It seems to have been taken for granted that the sinner had to make amends and bring about his own forgiveness by appealing to the one he had injured. This is startling in its logic to the average Christian, to whom it has never occurred that the one and only place to get forgiveness is from the individual sinned against.

The Huna system was definite, detailed, logical, and right to the point. It was simple and satisfactory because of a fuller knowledge of the complex and the low self that harbors the complex.

Another aspect of the atonement for sin is to be seen in the part played by sin in preventing normal contact between the low self and the High Self in one guilty of a sin. Since the kahunas held that one cannot injure the High Self in any way, and that the High Self has no part in cutting off the line of contact between itself and the low self, it follows that the low self, because of the sense of guilt it shares with the middle self, feels shame and is like a naughty child who avoids the presence of his parents.

It is thought that the low self has no sense of right and wrong of its own. It gets whatever idea it has about such matters from the middle self, whose reasoning power makes it possible for it to know right from wrong.

Because the low self is taught to accept blindly the decision of the middle self as to the right and wrong of any and all actions, it tends to develop fixations of guilt in a rather surprising fashion. Once a decision is reached as to the right or wrong of an action by the middle self, and that decision is given as a thought form to the low self for safekeeping, the fixation process is almost automatic. This is because the low self has been present and has sensed the solid physical action that caused the hurt to the one injured. This is a physical stimulus of a solid, tangible kind and when it has been observed by the low self, it has the effect of fixing the guilt sense immediately, rendering it a complex of much gravity. To drain off this complex, it becomes necessary to convince the middle self that amends have been made before there can be hope of getting the low self to release its fixed belief.

If a Christian, or other religionist, believes that he can sin against God by performing harmless acts he believes to be sins, such as the failure to attend Mass or the use of profanity, the fixation is not so important because it has not been accompanied by such a direct physical stimulus. In such cases a vague and general method of making amends is found in fasting and other forms of self-denial. As such things are excellent physical stimuli, they work well indeed in clearing up the lesser guilt fixations caused by the breaking of dogmatic religious commands. It is for a very good and practical reason that fasting and prayer have continued down the years to be the most used rites of all in seeking forgiveness for sins.

The low self is the "conscience," once it has received from the middle self training in what is right and wrong. This training is usually received in childhood at the instigation of watchful parents. Spankings do much to fix belief in right and wrong in the low self before the age of six.

When one is smitten by his conscience, he suffers an emotional reaction, not a logical one.

Conscience is *not* God-given or instinctive. It is simply the natural emotional reaction of a low self that has been taught that certain things are right and others wrong.

Only the middle self can sin. The animals in the jungle eat each other without sinning. The low self is an animal, even if associated with a middle self, and it is also incapable of sinning.

Contact between the High Self and the lower man comes through the low self and along the connecting cord of invisible shadowy body of the low self. If the low self is convinced that a man has been guilty of a wrong act, it feels shame and refuses to contact the High Self in the regular telepathic way across the connecting cord. Thus prayers are not delivered to the High Self. Its aid is not requested—and, under the law that man must be allowed to be a free agent in most things—no aid or guidance is given. The result is that the man blunders and gets into trouble. The kahunas spoke of this as a "blocking of the path." The "path," the "way," and the "light" are all words symbolic of the connection between the low self and the High Self. The kahuna words *la* and *ala* translate into these three words. The same use of these words as symbols is found in Christianity, but with less direct and definite meanings.

There seems to be a basic human urge to look for a god of some kind for help, or to try to appease the god if he seems to be angry and visits mankind with plagues and disasters.

Contact with the god is through a spoken prayer or request for attention. When prayers are not heard or not given attention, the suppliant resorts to various aids to prayer. The American Indians in our Southeast made elaborate sand paintings to symbolize the thing desired in prayer. Jews and Christians fast as an adjunct to prayer. There have also been cleansing rites that are supposed to make man sufficiently spotless to be acceptable before the god in prayer.

This cleansing process grew to be an elaborate ritual in most religions. Dogmas developed to teach that a man guilty of sin could not make his prayers heard unless he was first "forgiven" and ritually cleansed. Because the prayers of the good men got scarcely better answers than those of the wicked, there was a hunt for sins of which a good man might be guilty. The sin of omission and "original sin" were thus invented.

In the process of obtaining forgiveness for all forms of sin, and for the general purpose of pleasing the gods and thus gaining their favor, offerings were made. When the gods were appeased and the floods and plagues or individual difficulties ceased, there were thank-offerings, but these played a small part in the general scheme.

At the time of death, and the departure of the (almost universally recognized) soul of the man from his body, prayers and sacrifices were made by the living for the happiness and comfort of the departed in the "otherworld." The wicked might go to a hell; the average run of men might go to a place of temporary punishment. A deathbed ritual of prayer was commonly performed by a priest in as widely separated places as the Western seats of Christianity and the inner fastnesses of Tibet.

There nearly always arose a doctrine of a "chosen people" in the course of development of religions. The Jews were such a chosen people. The convert to Christianity became one of the chosen because he accepted Jesus as the focal point of his religious beliefs and depended upon an initiation into the ranks of the chosen through baptism, confirmation, and various similar rites, the end being to attain "salvation."

All the "salvations" were more or less alike in various religions. All need of being "saved" arose from a dogmatic belief that man in his normal state was lacking in some way or ways. He might have been "born in sin," or he might have been from a tribe that was not one of the "chosen" people. In India, where there was no vicarious atonement and resulting salvation through a belief in a "savior," the way of salvation was long and difficult. It led through thousands of incarnations while Karma was being lived down.

Nearly all religions eventually developed to the point where there was a dogmatic belief that a special building or place was necessary for proper prayer to the gods. From the altar and shrine grew the church and the temple.

While the primary purpose of religion was to appease the gods or to gain answers to prayers, there was also an idealistic concept frequently present in the belief that praise and worship of the gods was necessary. The primitives danced to entertain the god. They fed the god with burnt offerings and blood sacrifices—blood long being considered a probable source from which the god might derive sustenance (in Christianity the "blood of the Lamb" was necessary to appease God and get Him to allow a vicarious atonement for the sins of the world).

Dogmas multiplied and priesthoods flourished as each religion grew older. In the eternal search for a means of getting an answer to prayers from a god, some illogical and surprising practices developed: flagellation, castration, abhorrence of all normal sex relations, circumcision to prevent masturbation—the list is very long.

Huna may be called a science rather than a religion because it has almost nothing of religion in it. The High Self is not a god. It is the third spirit or part of man. It is no more divine than the low self or the middle self. It is simply a step advanced in mental powers and creative abilities. It is older and wiser and is parental in its attitude. It falls under the science of psychology, as certainly as do the low and middle (or subconscious and conscious) selves.

I have elected to call Huna a psycho-religious system for the reason that it includes so much that has always been considered a part of religion. However, I consider Huna a science in the strictest sense of the word. The kahunas knew nothing about gods. They admitted freely that it was probable that there were such Beings, but were honest in saying that they were convinced that the human mind would never be able to do more than imagine them—invent them in terms of lower humans.

In other words, the basic urge of older religions to appease gods or gain favors from them (religion plus magic) is replaced in Huna by the purely magical operation of prayer to the High Self for the purpose of gaining favors in the way of healing or bettering one's circumstances through a change in the predictable future.

Through the High Self, an appeal was made by the kahunas to the spirits able to control wind and weather, also to spirits in control of lower forms of life. (Pacts made in this manner prevented sharks in Hawaiian waters from attacking human beings—or at least that is the claim made by the kahunas of yesterday. In any event, the same breed of sharks that attacks men in other places is harmless in Hawaiian waters.)

Instead of feeding the gods with blood and burnt offerings, the kahunas understood the secret that lay behind the externals of all sacrifice. The High Self, in order to produce results on the physical plane, must draw from the physical body of earthly man sufficient vital force (*mana*) to use in the work.

The custom of building temples or shrines to aid in contacting the gods was not practiced by the genuine kahunas, although spurious kahunas of later times built temples of stone and offered sacrifices in vain efforts to get magical results.

The true kahunas needed no temples or shrines. They knew how to send telepathic messages to the High Self at will, regardless of place or conditions. They used no altar symbols, no incense or other mechanisms. (These things were reserved for use as physical stimuli to impress the low self when suggestion was being given for various purposes.)

The various rites used in religions to insure the dying a survival in spirit form and a certain amount of happiness as a spirit were unknown to the kahunas. They had no place in their matter-of-fact science for dogmas that demanded "salvation." Their teaching was simply that all people should know that the spirits of men survived death and that the memories and complexes of physical life were carried over into spirit life, making it advisable for the individual to rid himself of guilt complexes before death.

The kahunas believed that after death there was a continuation of growth and progression, the low self reincarnating as a middle self in due time and the middle self eventually rising to the level of the High Self, first learning to watch over lesser forms of life, and in the end, becoming the "utterly trustworthy parental spirit." The graduation, so to speak, of the low self to the level of a middle self is accomplished after death, during a period of inactivity resembling a long sleep. One is reminded of the worm that becomes a pupa, is inactive for a time, and then bursts forth as a butterfly.

The most important preparation for death must be done by the individual. He must reduce his guilt complexes to the minimum and free himself of dogmatic religious beliefs that will hinder him after he becomes a spirit. It is not necessary to spend more than a few months on the spirit plane before continuing the growth process, providing one knows the ropes as did the kahunas. Knowing Huna is knowing the ropes.

All we can take with us at the time of death is knowledge, and it should be the first duty of each of us to accumulate the correct "take-withable" knowledge by a careful study of the psycho-religions and the discarding of beliefs that cannot be substantiated.

At present we have before us only one basic and practical system, and that is Huna. I say this because Huna worked. It made practical mental healing as well as instant healing through the aid of the High Self. It made practical the system of gaining the aid of the High Self in changing the circumstances and the future of the individual.

Individuals may develop the ability to accumulate high charges of low-voltage vital force, then transfer it with thought forms of healing to those to be healed. Almost anyone can learn to use this low magic.

To learn to use the high magic, one has to get rid of hindering complexes, and this is difficult to do alone. This difficulty will be best met by group work in which one person assists another to unlock the path of contact with the High Self.

Of course, one can skirt around his own sin or guilt complexes and try for contact. Or, and this is a way open to all, the decision may be made as to just what is wanted, the prayer is formulated, and then repeated frequently with the command held over the low self to give the prayer and low *mana* to the High Self when automatic contact is made during sleep. It is a slow method, but better than the blind prayer offered without an understanding of its mechanism or of the High Self.

If one aspires to daily practice to learn to contact the High Self, there are several methods that will be of great help.

The first of these is the daily reading of writings that will bring before one the desirability of the undertaking and its complete possibility of success. We must never forget that we are creatures of massive mental habit. We get accustomed to thinking certain things in certain ways, and have to pull ourselves up by the bootstraps to prevent these habits from making us give up the practice before the first week is out. The low self is impressed by the printed page. It is a *physical stimulus*, and if the middle self believes the printed teachings to be correct or even workable, though illogical, the low self will gradually fall in line and accept the ideas.

Our complex beliefs can be a help as well as a hindrance. It is, however, necessary for us to pull ourselves together mentally at daily intervals and make a close and critical examination of our many pertinent beliefs. We may have to dwell daily on the great Huna truth, which is for us the epitome of liberation, the truth that we cannot sin against Higher Beings, and that there is no sin other than hurting another human being.

No hurt, no sin! Shout it from the housetops every hour for a year if need be. At all costs gain the salvation of liberation from false dogmas of sin. Or, if you fail in that, humor your complexed low self and cease to do the things it stubbornly and blindly insists on considering sinful.

Huna is not crystallized and set and dead. It is a living, practical system that holds fast to the proven, while reaching out eagerly to inspect anything new and promising. But those who aspire to benefit by the ancient discoveries that comprise the heart of the secret must also be open and ready for change.

The low self is the custodian of all our memories and habits of thought and belief. It stores all our memories and thoughts in its low shadowy body, and presides over them stubbornly and illogically. It takes time and practice, reading and rereading, to bring it into line and keep it there—ready to make contact with the High Self.

An indication that we are entering a new period in our progress toward world civilization is to be seen in the step from the agelong secrecy of Huna to an open knowledge available to all. The cult of secrecy fostered priesthoods, and priesthoods fostered special privileges, the victims being laymen.

While there will be those who possess certain natural talents that will enable them to learn to use the kahuna methods and thus to become healers, there will no longer be a bind of secrecy and mystery about the methods used. The layman, while perhaps not aspiring to become a professional healer of body or purse, will be able to read the literature and know the principles of the new psycho-religious system.

This system, while based on ancient fundamentals, will undoubtedly move ahead very rapidly when modern discoveries and laboratory methods are brought into use. For instance, we can now measure and show on graph paper the electrovital impulses that move through the brain and we should someday know more about the *mana* of the kahunas than they ever knew. This is a machine age, and it is safe to predict that our recovery of the knack of using Huna will be tied up with machines in various ways, as we improve steadily on the ancient practices.

The effect of a general knowledge of Huna on world social structures will be fascinating to watch. Because we have had no sufficiently detailed and workable psycho-religious knowledge, we have had no way of unifying our ideas on these subjects. With Huna acting as a criterion and catalytic agent, the choas of ideas in these fields can be reduced to order.

Without the science of psycho-religion, we have lived like animals while prating about high ideals and brotherhood, unable to do anything about these ideals because we could not understand ourselves. We have not known what we were, why we were here, or where we were going. In other words, this department of life has been, and is, disorganized and jumbled. We hurt each other, and unite in groups and nations to make war on other groups and nations—a pretty spectacle for intelligent beings at our stage of development.

If we can settle the basics in this field of knowledge, we shall be on the road to apply that knowledge to the betterment of humanity, as we now apply what we know to agriculture and animal husbandry. By freeing ourselves from the dogmas of outmoded religions, we will be able to take sensible and practical steps in a forward direction, replacing disorganized growth under the dispensation of the animal-like low self by the dispensation of the middle self aided by the High Self.

It is as if our civilization had long been allowed to grow as a form of wildlife, creating tangled forest and jungle growths, fields choked with weeds, and with the ever-present danger of fire wiping all away. The "wild growth" can be replaced with planned and ordered fields and forests, so to speak, with firebreaks protecting cultivated sections from those still left wild.

Union is strength, prosperity, and safety. The High Beings ruling the ants and bees demonstrate this. Rugged individualism and disunion, as represented by predatory animals that are themselves in constant danger of being eaten, symbolize the stage of growth in which the hard lessons of life under free will must be learned. Following that stage comes the one we have been missing so long: the stage in which man returns to a united and cooperative effort, still possessing his free will, but using it in the correct relation to his fellow men—and, above all, in the correct relation to the High Selves, whence come both help and guidance.

We are at the turning of the road at last, and the prospect that lies ahead, even when seen mistily through the veil of time, appears to be very bright indeed.

15

Publications Devoted to Huna Research

For several years, until his recent serious illness, Max Freedom Long and his Huna Research Association issued *Huna Vistas,* a regular bimonthly bulletin that covered news of Huna research, book reviews, and reports on healing projects. The H.R.A. published six books containing detailed instructions and aids for developing Huna magic. Each of the books was authored by Max Freedom Long, who drew upon his several years of extensive research in investigating the multifaceted mysteries of the kahunas.

The Secret Science Behind Miracles (1948) is the basic work on Huna magic. In this book, Long reveals how the kahunas of Hawaii were able to perform apparent miracles of instant healing, attested to glimpses of the future, and documented accounts of fire-walking and control of natural forces. Long details precisely how he discovered the clues to the secret knowledge in the roots of significant words and explains in clear language how the kahunas mastered a wide range of psychic phenomena.

Five years after the release of *The Secret Science Behind Miracles,* the H.R.A. published Long's *The Secret Science at Work,* a collection of methods that had been found most effective for the use of Huna by the average person. A few years later, in answer to increasing demands from an ever-growing circle of students, Long and the H.R.A. published *Growing into Light,* a book that could be used for daily reading to help keep the student's mind on Huna ideas and principles.

For *Self-Suggestion and the New Huna Theory of Mesmerism and Hypnosis'* Max Freedom Long drew upon the proffered assistance of devoted friends in compiling a volume of tried and tested methods of putting Huna principles to beneficial application. The techniques in this volume are said to swiftly bring the subliminal, or low self, to obey instructions and perform its vital role in making full use of Huna. Long's *Psychometric Analysis* is another effort slanted toward offering Huna as a means of putting ESP to practical use.

The most recent publication of the H.R.A. is undoubtedly its most controversial. In *The Huna Code in Religions,* Max Freedom Long offers his thesis that the code of the kahunas was grafted onto many passages in the New Testament in order to convey the inner teachings of Huna. What Long presents in this provocative book is an entirely different slant and, perhaps, insight into the nature and work of Jesus. Not content to ferret out Huna code words in the New Testament, Long carefully analyzed the Apocrypha, the Old Testament, the gnostic and mystery writings, the teachings of yoga, and the secrets of esoteric Buddhism.

In Long's words: "The four Gospels became a mine of information which was so strange and unexpected that a burst of new light began to illuminate teachings which had been incomplete for centuries."

In a letter to this author, Long confided that he had originally intended to title the work, *What Jesus Taught in Secret.*

"Down the centuries there has been a tradition that there was a secret teaching in the *Bible,* and several people have concocted arbitrary codes and written about them and sold their stuff," Long wrote. "Readers of those books are, naturally, suspicious of any new claims to have broken the code, but in my *Huna Code in Religions,* I have been at a considerable amount of pains, so to speak, to give the selections photographically reproduced from the old Hawaiian dictionary where the code is easily seen, once one knows what to look for: 1. Words with a number of meanings, and 2. Words standing for things like water and seeds and breath, which came to symbolize several parts of the ancient set of beliefs and practices."

Appendix I

The Ten Basic Elements in Kahuna Magic

By now the reader will have a general picture of the ancient psychology and lore of the Huna system of magic. "It must always be kept in mind," Max Freedom Long reminds us, "that there are three sets of three things, and a physical body." Following are the abbreviated lists that Max Freedom Long has prepared to assist the reader in checking over the basic elements and principles of kahuna magic.

The Ten Elements in Kahuna Magic or Psychology

I.   Three spirits which compose the man (living or deceased).

A. The subconscious. Remembers but has defective reason. Creates all emotions.

B. The conscious. Cannot remember but has full reasoning power.

C. The superconscious. It has a form of mentation by which it knows by a process of "realizing." It knows the past, the present, and as much of the future as has been crystallized or definitely planned, created, or projected on its level.

II. The three voltages of vital force (mana) used by the three spirits of man.

A. The body waves or low-voltage vital electrical force. It is used by the subconscious and can flow over threads of shadowy body substance (aka—similiar to "astral cords"). It can carry chemical substances with it as it flows from person to person. It can take the form of magnetism and can be stored in wood and other porous substances. A large discharge of this low-voltage vital force commanded by the "will" can exert a paralyzing effect or a mesmeric effect resulting in unconsciousness, sleep, and the rigid or cataleptic state.

B. The brain waves or vital force of the next higher voltage, used by the conscious mind spirit in us in all its thinking and "willing" activities. Used at will, it can be mesmeric or hypnotic force, provided that a thought form is introduced into the mind of the subject. It cannot travel over the shadowy substance threads, as can the lower voltage. (Or at least it seems not to do so.)

C. The high voltage of vital force (not discovered by science as yet), that is thought by the kahunas to be used by the superconscious for its various purposes. It is of the atom-smashing voltage of electrical energy, in all probability.

III.   The invisible or shadowy substance (etheric or astral) bodies in which the three spirits composing man reside. The lower two usually interblend with each other and with the body during life. They remain interblended after death unless separated by some unfortunate circumstance.

A. The shadowy body of the subconscious. It is the most dense of the three. It is of such a nature that it sticks to whatever we touch (or perhaps see or hear), and when removed from the contact, draws out a long invisible thread of itself which connects one with the thing contacted, in a form of semi-permanent union. (It is not known how permanent this thread or the main body itself may be, but it seems to survive far longer than dense physical substances.) All things were supposed by the kahunas to have a shadowy body, be they crystals, plants, animals, fabricated articles, men, or gods—even thoughts (the latter being very important to the magical system and its practices). This substance is an ideal conductor of vital electrical force or currents, and can be used as a storage place for it. When heavily charged with the low voltage of the force, it becomes rigid and firm enough to be used as a "hand" or instrument to move or affect physical objects—as in table-tipping, etc.

B. The shadowy body of the conscious mind spirit of man is less dense than that of the subconscious. It seems not to be sticky or to pull out into threads. It may or may not be a conductor of low-voltage vital force, but undoubtedly is a conductor of the middle voltage—its own peculiar voltage as used in its form of mentation and "will." It forms the ghostly body in which the spirit functions as a spirit after death.

C. The shadowy body of the superconscious spirit of man. The superconscious is supposed to reside in this invisible and very light body at all times, seldom making direct contact with the physical body by entering it. By analogy, it is supposed to have characteristics somewhat resembling the shadowy bodies of the two lower spirits.

Simplified Terms for the Ten Elements in the Ancient Psychological System

I.   Low spirit or low self: the subconscious. A separate spirit.

II.   Low *mana* or low voltage of vital force. Used by the low spirit.

III. Low *aka* or low shadowy body (low astral or etheric double) of the low self.

IV.   Middle spirit of self: the conscious mind, spirit, or entity. It is a separate spirit and not a permanent part of the low self.

V.   Middle *mana* or middle voltage of vital force. Used only by the middle spirit.

VI.   The middle *aka* or middle shadowy body, inhabited by the middle spirit.

VII. The High Self or Spirit: the superconscious. A separate spirit or self connected distantly with the low and middle selves, and acting as an "overself," or parental guardian spirit.

VIII. The High *Aka* or high shadowy body of the High Self, in which it lives.

IX.   The High *Mana* or high voltage of vital force, used by the High Self or High Spirit.

X.   The body: the physical body which is entered by the low and middle spirits or selves in their *aka* bodies and used by them during life. The

High Self is distantly connected to the physical body, probably, for the most part, by *aka* threads issued by the low self from its shadowy body.

Corresponding Terms in Hawaiian

I.   Low self: *unihipili.*

II.   Low vital force: *mana.*

III. Low shadowy body: *kino-aka.*

IV.   Middle self or spirit: *uhane.*

V.   Middle voltage of vital force: *mana-mana* (a symbol, meaning "to spread out as a vine"). (Doubling the root often indicates an increase in the strength of the meaning.)

VI.   Middle shadowy body: *kino-aka.* (No differentiation of term.)

VII. High Self or Spirit: *Aumakua* (meaning older, parental, and perfectly trustworthy spirit). There are a number of other names also to indicate the High Self in its various activities, and it is obvious that the kahunas paid it much attention.

VIII. High voltage of vital force: *mana-loa* (meaning strongest or greatest force). The symbol of the High Self was the sun, and its force was symbolized by the light.

IX.   High shadowy body: *kino-aka,* with no differentiation of the term as applied to the two lower spirits, although there seems to have been some use of symbolic terms to indicate it. The Berber kahuna thought its symbol was the moon.

X.   The physical body: *kino.*

Appendix II

The study of Huna is an ongoing project. Your reading of this text has probably whet your appetite for more research of your own. Below is a partial list of publications you can refer to in rounding out your own education.

Finch, William J., *The Pendulum and the Possession*, Phoenix: Esoteric Publications, 1973.

Hoffman, Enid, *Huna: A Beginners Guide*. Rockport, Mass: Para Research, 1976.

King, Serge, *Mana Physics*. New York: Baraka Books' 1978.

Long, Max Freedom, *Growing into Light*. Santa Monica: DeVorss, 1955.

Long, Max Freedom, *The Huna Code in Religions*. Santa Monica: DeVorss, 1965.

Long, Max Freedom, *Psychometric Analysis*. Santa Monica: DeVorss, 1959.

Long, Max Freedom, *The Secret Science at Work*. Santa Monica: DeVorss, 1953.

Long, Max Freedom, *The Secret Science Behind Miracles*. Santa Monica: DeVorss, 1948.

Long, Max Freedom, *Self-Suggestion and the New Huna Theory of Mesmerism and Hypnosis*. Santa Monica: DeVorss, 1958.

McBride, L.R., *The Kahuna, Versatile Mystics of Old Hawaii*. Hilo, Hawaii: Petroglyph Press.

Westlake, Aubrey T., *The Pattern of Health: A Search for a Greater Understanding of the Life Force in Health and Disease*. Berkeley: Shambhala Publications, 1961.

In addition, the Huna Research Associates is carrying on the work of Max Freedom Long. They can be reached care of Dr. E. Otha Wingo, Director, Huna Research, 126 Camelia Drive, Cape Girardeau, Missouri 63701.

Index

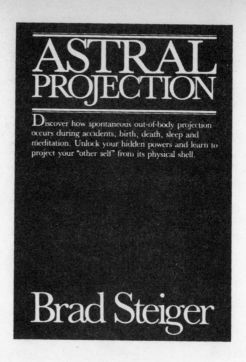

Discover how spontaneous out-of-body projection occurs during accidents, birth, death, sleep and meditation. Unlock your hidden powers and learn to project your "other self" from its physical shell.

Brad Steiger

ASTRAL PROJECTION

Brad Steiger

Parapsychological researchers have established that one of every one hundred persons has experienced out-of-body projection (OBE). These experiences are not limited to any single type of person, but rather they cross all typical boundaries.

In *Astral Projection*, Brad Steiger, investigates the phenomenon of OBE and correlates those events into broad categories for analysis and explanation. In his clear and non-sensational style, Steiger relates how these spontaneous experiences occur and when they are likely to re-occur. In addition to the standard and well-documented categories of spontaneous astral projection at times of stress, sleep, death and near-death, Steiger devotes considerable time to the growing evidence for conscious out-of-body experiences, where the subject deliberately seeks to cast his or her spirit out of the physical shell.

Along with his study of astral projection, Steiger sets guidelines for astral travellers, tells them the dangers they may face and how this type of psychic experience might be used for medical diagnosis, therapy and self-knowledge.

Author Brad Steiger is your guide to controlling astral projection and using it for your own benefit.

ISBN 0-914918-36-2
234 pages, 6½" x 9¼", paper $12.95

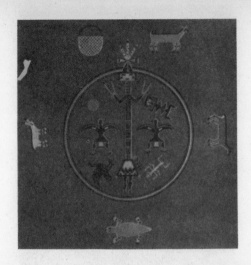

INDIAN MEDICINE POWER

Brad Steiger

According to Brad Steiger, medicine power, a way of life elemental to Native American heritage and contemporary religious practice, may well be the unique mystical experience and the proper spiritual path for our continent. At the core of medicine power is the quest for wisdom of mind and body. Men and women pursuing this quest are often great healers, but the true meaning of the term "medicine" extends beyond the arts of healing to include clairvoyance, precognition and unity with nature and the great spirit.

Indian Medicine Power includes extensive interviews with contemporary medicine men and women from numerous tribes. Steiger himself was initiated into the medicine lodge of the Wolf Clan of the Seneca tribe, given the name of Hat-yas-swas (He Who Testifies) and charged with the search and sharing of universal truths.

The truths of medicine power shared in this book include the nature and importance of the vision quest, the belief in total partnership with the World of Spirits, awareness of one's place in the web of life and the power of walking in balance with the earth.

As Donna Linstead, a member of the Cree Tribe and professor of Native American Studies, says in her introduction: "*Indian Medicine Power* provides each reader with a path from yesterday to tomorrow that allows for individual growth, awareness, and an accessibility to the ancient mysteries that continue to be practiced today. Brad Steiger has demonstrated an uncommon insight into the sacred belief systems of the Amerindian."

ISBN 0-914918-65-6
240 pages, paper

$12.95

A reporter's encounters with ghosts who walk, speak, move objects and even kill. How spirits haunt the scenes of their violent death. Here's convincing proof of a spirit world that exists all around us. With an introduction by Hans Holzer.

Brad Steiger

TRUE GHOST STORIES

A Psychic Researcher's Hunt
for Evidence of Hauntings

Brad Steiger

Brad Steiger's years of research into the infinite expanse of the spirit world is now available in this fascinating compilation of verified hauntings. These are not only the classic ghostly manifestations often discussed in paranormal literature, but also cases Steiger has researched, often using well-known mediums as contact points with the ethereal energies. *True Ghost Stories* does not stop at just relating the details of ghostly hauntings, it goes beyond other books on ghosts and hauntings to present the prevailing hypotheses about spirits in a scientific, yet highly readable manner.

The author investigates and explains three predominant theories that claim such manifestations are "telepathic infection," "idea patterns" or "psychic ether." Steiger concludes that no single one of these theories should be held dominant, but then again, none should exclude the other. *True Ghost Stories* proves the existence of ghosts and reveals significant facts and features of their nature. This new book leaves the reader with the chilling realization that we have yet to fully understand ghosts; more can be learned only through future contacts with the spirits.

ISBN 0-914918-35-4
220 pages, 6½" x 9¼", paper

$7.95

HUNA: A Beginner's Guide

Enid Hoffman

As author Enid Hoffman recalls, "I began to feel with rising excitement that I was on to something very valuable and real. I learned that this concept was at the bottom of all the practices of the Kahuna. Their miracles and magic were the result of their profound knowledge of energies and substances, visible and invisible. This knowledge enabled them to control their life experiences instead of having events control them, and made it possible for them to assist others to do so. I became aware that they were expert psychologists with a thorough understanding of human nature. Their understanding of interpersonal relationships and relationships between the selves and the physical world gave them incredible power.

"For me, these were very exciting realizations, holding the potential for everyone to grow in knowledge and power. My enthusiasm grew because I knew that if the Kahuna had done it, we could do it by studying the Huna concept, practicing their techniques until we were as skilled as they. Then we would be able to produce miracles, too."

Centuries ago, the Kahuna, the ancient Hawaiian miracle workers, discovered the fundamental pattern of energy-flow in the universe. Their secrets of psychic and intrapsychic communication, refined and enriched by modern scientific research, are now revealed in this practical, readable book. Learn to talk directly to your own unconscious selves and others. It could change your life.

ISBN 0-914918-03-6
220 pages, 6½" x 9¼", paper

$12.95

DEVELOP YOUR PSYCHIC SKILLS

Enid Hoffman

Psychic skills are as natural to human beings as walking and talking and are much more easily learned. Here are the simple directions *and* the inside secrets from noted teacher and author Enid Hoffman.

Develop Your Psychic Skills gives you a broad overview of the whole field of psychic experiences. The exercises and practices given in this book are enjoyable and easy to do. Use them to strengthen and focus your own natural abilities and turn them into precise, coordinated skills. You'll be amazed at the changes that begin to happen in your life as you activate the right hemisphere of your brain, the intuitive, creative, psychic half, which has been ignored for so long.

This book shows you how your natural psychic powers can transform your life when you awaken the other half of your brain. It teaches you techniques for knowing what others are doing, feeling and thinking. You can see what the future holds and explore past lives. You can learn to locate lost objects and people. You can become a psychic healer. It is all open to you.

Develop occasional hunches into definite foreknowledge. Sharpen wandering fantasies and daydreams into clear and accurate pictures of events in other times and places. Choose what you want to do with your life by developing your psychic skills. When you finish this book you'll realize, as thousands of others have using Enid Hoffman's techniques, that the day you began to develop your psychic skills was the day you began to become fully conscious, fully creative and fully alive.

ISBN: 0-914918-29-X
192 pages, 6½" X 9¼", paper $9.95

EXPAND YOUR PSYCHIC SKILLS

Enid Hoffman

In this sequel to her best-selling *Develop Your Psychic Skills*, Hoffman shows you how to use your inate psychic abilities to improve your daily life and your relationships with other beings. Huna concepts, along with dozens of techniques, exercises, games and meditations are included to help you fully utilize your inner resources. Psychic healing, working with crystals and gemstones, communicating telepathically with people and animals, heightening creative powers, and eliminating old behaviors that are interfering with your personal growth are just a few of the areas covered.

ISBN: 0-914918-72-9
144 pages, 6½" X 9¼", paper

$9.95

COMPLETE
MEDITATION

Steve Kravette

Complete Meditation presents a broad range of metaphysical concepts and meditation techniques in the same direct, easy-to-assimilate style of the author's best-selling *Complete Relaxation*. Personal experience is the teacher and this unique book is your guide. The free, poetic format leads you through a series of exercises that build on each other, starting with breathing patterns, visualization exercises and a growing confidence that meditation is easy and pleasurable. Graceful illustrations flow along with the text.

    Complete Meditation is for readers at all levels of experience. It makes advanced metaphysics and esoteric practices accessible without years of study of the literature, attachment to gurus or initiation into secret societies. Everyone can meditate, everyone is psychic, and with only a little attention everyone can bring oneself and one's circumstances into harmony.

    Experienced meditators will appreciate the more advanced techniques, including more sophisticated breathing patterns, astral travel, past-life regression, and much more. All readers will appreciate being shown how ordinarily "boring" experiences are really illuminating gateways into the complete meditation experience. Whether you do all the exercises or not, just reading this book is a pleasure.

    Complete meditation can happen anywhere, any time, in thousands of different ways. A candle flame, a daydream, music, sex, a glint of light on your ring. In virtually any circumstances. *Complete Meditation* shows you how.

ISBN 0-914918-28-1
320 pages, 6½" x 9¼", paper, $12.95

COMPLETE RELAXATION

Steve Kravette

Complete Relaxation is unique in its field because, unlike most relaxation books, it takes a completely relaxed approach to its subject. You will find a series of poetic explorations interspersed with text and beautifully drawn illustrations designed to put you in closer touch with yourself and the people around you. *Complete Relaxation* is written for all of you: your body, your mind, your emotions, your spirituality, your sexuality—the whole person you are and are meant to be.

As you read this book, you will begin to feel yourself entering a way of life more completely relaxed than you ever thought possible. Reviewer Ben Reuven stated in the *Los Angeles Times*, "*Complete Relaxation* came along at just the right time—I read it, tried it; it works."

Some of the many areas that the author touches upon are: becoming aware, instant relaxation, stretching, hatha yoga, Arica, bioenergetics, Tai chi, dancing, and the Relaxation Reflex.

Mantras, meditating, emotional relaxation, holding back and letting go, learning to accept yourself, business relaxation, driving relaxation.

Family relaxation, nutritional relaxation, spiritual relaxation, sensual relaxation, massage and sexual relaxation. *Complete Relaxation* is a book the world has been tensely, nervously, anxiously waiting for. Here it is. Read it and relax.

ISBN 0-914918-14-1
310 pages, 6½" x 9¼", paper $10.95

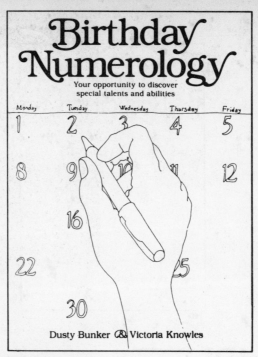

BIRTHDAY NUMEROLOGY

by Dusty Bunker and Victoria Knowles

One of the unique things about you is the day on which you were born. In *Birthday Numerology*, well-known numerologist Dusty Bunker and psychic counselor Victoria Knowles combine their knowledge of numerology, symbolism and psychic development to present a clear and coherent presentation of how the day you were born affects your personality.

Unlike other methods of divination, the beauty of this book lies in its simple and direct presentation of the meaning behind personal numbers. Rather than having to perform complicated calculations, all you need to do is know your birthday. The book is uncannily accurate, written in a warm and engaging style and, above all, is easy to use.

The introductory chapters discuss the foundation and validity of numerology and will help you discover why the date of your birth is crucial in determining your personality. From there, *Birthday Numerology* examines the traits and characteristics inherent in people born on each day of the month.

Dusty Bunker and Vikki Knowles have written a book that is much more than just a delineation of various personalities, it is truly a guidebook to your journey through the 31 days.

ISBN 0-914918-39-7
225 pages, 6½" x 9¼", paper

$13.95

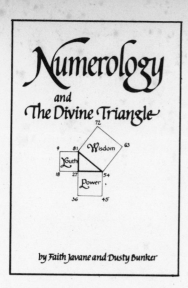

NUMEROLOGY & THE DIVINE TRIANGLE

Faith Javane & Dusty Bunker

Now in its fourth printing, this major work embodies the life's work of Faith Javane, one of America's most respected numerologists, and her student and co-author Dusty Bunker, a teacher and columnist on metaphysical topics.

Part I introduces esoteric numerology. Topics include: the digits 1 through 9; how to derive your personal numbers from your name and date of birth; how to chart your life path; the symbolism of each letter in the alphabet; the life of Edgar Cayce, and more.

Part II delineates the numbers 1 through 78 and, illustrated with the Rider-Waite Tarot deck, synthesizes numerology, astrology and the Tarot. *Numerology & The Divine Triangle* is number one in its field.

ISBN 0-914918-10-9
280 pages, 6½" x 9¼", paper $14.95

NUMEROLOGY AND YOUR FUTURE

Dusty Bunker

In her second book, Dusty Bunker stresses the predictive side of numerology. Personal cycles, including yearly, monthly and even daily numbers are explored as the author presents new techniques for revealing future developments. Knowledge of these cycles will help you make decisions and take actions in your life.

In addition to the extended discussion of personal cycles, the numerological significance of decades is analyzed with emphasis on the particular importance of the 1980s. Looking toward the future, the author presents a series of examples from the past, particularly the historical order of American presidents in relation to keys from the Tarot, to illustrate the power of numbers. Special attention is paid to the twenty-year death cycle of the presidents, as well as several predictions for the presidential elections.

ISBN 0-914918-18-4
235 pages, 6½" x 9¼", paper $12.95